"Movin' On"

Dorothy James Hayes:

Slogans to Live By

Dedicated to:

Dorothy, herself, because her story needs to be told,

The people who know her, so benefit from her life and its story being told

And finally, all else who just need to know.

Part I:

From the

South

Table of Contents:

Part I—From the South

"Prologue"

"Even Birds Must Land"

"Money does not Matter, only Family"

"Grew up Black"

"Just don't know what Tomorrow Brings"

"Always Runnin'"

"Too Old to Vote"

"Gotta Keep Going"

"Gotta Survive"

"Life is what you Make It"

"Little House on the Prairie"

"Prologue"

It was hot and humid, that day. Even though it was November, it continued to be hot and humid. It often remained this way in Mississippi at almost any time of the year. That sticky cloud of moisture just clung over the acres of rural fields that then, in 1924, still may, and had for decades before, hung over this agrarian landscape. The sun pushed its bright face through the clouds, down on the miles of cotton, tobacco, and vegetable fields as it always had. Even the faces in the fields, Black faces, could have been planting and sowing as centuries before, in slavery. Today, though, they sharecropped. Technically, they owned their land segment and its crops. Still, half of all went to the actual land owner, and all knew that little had truly changed.

Truly little had changed in rural Mississippi since the days of slavery, particularly in 1924, and maybe even today. The emotional and political climate of this place and time had always been one of hot weather and tempers with humid weather and "sticky," unchanging moods, similar to that climate. The Twenties, in the metropolitan areas, may have been the "Roaring Twenties," as they called it, when "bob" haircuts were the rage, Flappers were doing the "Charlestown," and even Ragtime and Jazz music celebrated Blacks as part of the Harlem Renaissance. However, these rural Blacks knew nothing of this modern glamour and city life. Most just knew years of toil and hours of work. The survival of farming was all that was around them. Even their appearance was one of poverty: shoeless children and homespun clothing, handed down as one child grew out of it, given to the next one in line. Scarves, not more stylish and expensive hats, were what covered their tightly-tied corn-rolled braids.

Although symbols of meager means and hard work were apparent in their attire, and Black features dominated their faces, strength and courage could still be found stealing out from their demeanors. This strength may be hidden from the Whites, who still required down-cast eyes with a bowed glance and nod. However, this strength was evident and illuminated secretly in their homes and with their families. Yes, the Blacks of that Era were surviving, as the Blacks of today still are. One Mississippi sharecropper family, in particular, had reason to celebrate and be grateful for their existence, during this year's Thanksgiving season. Even with three other children, their fourth, a girl, was welcomed whole-heartedly to their home on November 24, 1924, and they called her Dorothy Nell James.

"Even Birds Must Land"

Dorothy was born, into this other place and time, as if a piece of history. Literally, she may have been born as part of the so-called "Industrial-Revolutionized" Twentieth Century of the 1920s. She was even technically a citizen of the modern and free United States of America. However,

Dorothy was actually born in Centerville, Mississippi, still under the rule of "Jim Crow." Mississippi was considered legitimately by some, then and now, as one of the most prejudiced and backward States in the Union. Her family farm was not a traditional farm of the North or West, but a sharecropper farm of the South, created from the previous plantations of yesteryear. They sharecropped for a cheating plantation owner who instead of taking the usual 1/1, actually took two barrels for every one grown of the planted cotton, plus corn, potatoes, beans, peas, cabbage, collard greens, and onions, making Dorothy a sharecropper of yesteryear, too.

Dorothy's sharecropper youth may have been spent on a once-White man's Plantation, but the days of luxurious Plantations had disappeared and were long since gone. That land once was one of flowing, green terrain complete with cash crops, acres and acres of soil, the property of one single White man who owned the Blacks who worked there. Instead, this land was divided into smaller, less fertile segments now "owned" by the Blacks who worked them. The clay soil seemed to bear less, with fewer hands to till it, anymore. The animals were even more bedraggled and thin, less valuable than they would have been in the by-gone days. The cattle, also not as numerous, were not pedigreed show beasts but only "milkers" and "haulers." However, they were still given names and places in the family. Even today, Dorothy still remembers growing up with a family favorite, a cow named Nellie. That memory was not only nostalgic, though. After owning this cow, no family member was allowed to call Dorothy by her middle name of Nell, especially as a nickname. Later, when grown, Dorothy also removed the middle name of Nell from her birth certificate, so as to not share it with a cow.

When Dorothy entered this world of crops and cattle, her paternal grandparents had already passed into the next, less-tiring world. Their departure came after years of struggle and pain, "slaving," literally on a Southern plantation. Her maternal grandparents, one a part- Indian blooded woman, Mama Lizzie, who was truly magnificent to behold, and her totally blind husband, Papa Levi, were Dorothy's only family connection to the not-so-distant past of a reconstructed South. Dorothy specifically remembers a picture she still has of her grandmother. This woman was truly something to see with her distinct beard (Dorothy never knew why a woman would have one and why it would only be trimmed at her death) and long, dark braids falling down her back. Because her grandmother looked so much like a man, Dorothy's descendants still ask Dorothy if she was scared of Mama Lizzie. "No," would be Dorothy's certain reply because "she was my grandmother, my kin," Dorothy would add. In one of Dorothy's oldest photographs, Mama Lizzie is pictured rocking in an old sagging "straw" rocking chair sitting on a thread-bare pillow rocking as she "moaned" and sang. After her grandmother had passed, the rocking chair just seemed to collapse, and even in those years of "use it up, make it do, or fix it up," it was necessary to "throw it out."

When Dorothy told of her grandmother, Mama Lizzie, Dorothy also spoke of cabbage and rice. Mama Lizzie always cooked cabbage and rice for every meal and always together. Then and now, Dorothy loved rice, but sometimes all that cabbage got to be "tiresome." Dorothy loved to spend the night at Mama Lizzie's house, even if the cabbage got to be a "little too much." At Grandmother's house, she, just like folk singer John Denver, could sleep in Grandmother's feather bed. She also claimed Papa Levi's feather pillow as Grandpa was "gone" by then. Sleeping in that feather bed, with that feather pillow, was pure heaven for Dorothy because to "sleep in" at Mama Lizzie's became one of Dorothy's fondest childhood memories. In fact, Mama Lizzie would ask her daughter, Dorothy's mother, if she just worked Dorothy "too long and hard" because "all she does at my house is sleep." Dorothy also specifically remembers eating, and always "cleaning her plate," including all the cabbage, at Grandmother's house. This was simply because in "tough times," like being Black in the South, "called for tough measures," never wasting anything, and especially not wasting food. In spite of these tough times, Grandmother, Mama Lizzie still kept her faith. She believed until the day she died that God keeps his promise to us in the Holy Bible to never give any of us more than we can handle. She would often quote, "…God is faithful, who will not suffer you to be tempted above that ye are able; but will with the temptation also make a way to escape, that ye may be able to bear it" (1 Corinthians 10:13).

Mama Lizzie, Mama Lizzie's brother, Uncle Robert, and Mama Lizzie's husband, Papa Levi, and Dorothy's "already passed" father's parents were all slaves.

Aside from them being slaves, Dorothy knew very little else of her father's parents, except that her father's mother was full-blooded Indian and named Carolina. All of these family members, on both sides, had only been emancipated through the not-so-recent Northern victory in the Civil War.

Dorothy's mother, Idora McCraine, carried with her the blood and wisdom of her maternal ancestors, and she would often quote them. Therefore, Dorothy grew up hearing many wise philosophies from the past: Such statements as "Even the bird that is flying high has to come down to the ground for food and water" were common-place. Dorothy was taught to translate this wisdom into part of her existence. She learned to soar to the heavens, with the essential education to do so, but to stay close enough to the ground to do the necessary work for food and survival on this earth. Idora also practiced the lessons that she preached; she had the education of a new day and the work ethic of an old day. In spite of difficulty and rarity, Idora had learned to read and write. Idora passed this same requirement for literacy onto her children, although her husband, and Dorothy's father, Joseph James, died illiterate.

Because of his illiteracy, Joseph James, only knew the fields and field work, although he was not exceptional at some of the other agrarian tasks common to men of his time. Dorothy believes this was probably because he was extremely soft-hearted. Joseph was not a gifted hunter, like his sons, because when he shot, even just for food, he would shoot the animal over and over again to make sure it was dead, literally pulverizing the meat before being taken home for food. Because of this, Dorothy's mother became the family butcher. Ironically, Idora actually did more of the farm butchering than Joseph did. To slaughter the goats (one of their most frequently butchered beasts), Idora would cover the animals' heads with a burlap sack. This was a common "goat slaughtering" technique so the goat would not watch its own demise. Goats are such "sensitive creatures" Dorothy was told. "If allowed to watch their head being chopped off, they would whine and cry so much to make the process almost impossible for anyone to complete, no matter how senseless the killer was," she added. All told, Idora came to do many of the manly tasks of the James household.

One of the essential lessons Idora taught her children was that even with "faces of black" that they must "look over and move on." In other words, Dorothy learned to not seek revenge, but see the beauty beyond, instead. Though, Dorothy has also said, just as Bessie Delany, a Black author in Having Our Say, said: "This race business does get under my skin. I have suffered a lot in my life because of it. If you asked me how I endured it, I would have to say it was because I had a good upbringing. My parents did not encourage me to be bitter. If they had, I'd have been so mean it would have killed my spirit a long, long time ago" (105). Specifically, Dorothy credits her mother with the reason she is not racist and could never be ruined by hate. Mother taught, and acted upon the philosophy, that to love was to be Christian and to hate to be a Hypocrite. After all, the Bible says, "Love one another as I have loved you…" (John 13: 34).

It was because of facing this hate that Idora reminded her eight sons and daughters "where you're going, I've been." Not only did she know of Southern discrimination, but also of hard work. She even had the big, rough hands, and feet, of a laborer. Today, Dorothy also has the big hands and feet (size 11 shoe) of a "hard-working woman." These are her biggest physical features, in fact. Just like Scarlett O'Hara, in "Gone with the Wind," manual laboring women, Black and White, could always be told by their hands (Mitchell 578-579). Also, Idora was always in the kitchen, wearing that symbol of kitchen help, an apron. Years later, Little Idora, as Dorothy was often called, after her mother, would also be known for always being in the kitchen, wearing an apron, and enduring years of hard work.

However, Dorothy's mother had one characteristic that Dorothy was never able to master. Idora was able to carry a large round water bucket, full, on her head. She did this daily as she brought water to the workers in the sharecropper's fields. Dorothy often tried to copy her mother's example by trying to carry a bucket, empty even, on her head. However, the empty bucket, never mind full, always fell from her head. Family members would tease Dorothy that her head was "too round for the task." Overall, Dorothy was, and still is, extremely flattered to be compared to her mother. In her own words, Dorothy states the following compliment about her much-admired parent: "I may be a strong, hardworking woman. If I am, it is because my mother taught me how to be one. I am very proud and grateful for that."

Interestingly, her mother, Idora, when she had occasion to relax, would always smoke a pipe with Father, Joseph. She was even described to be that "jolly old soul," just like Old King Cole. Both smoked in the house, while no one else was allowed to. Because of this "in-the-house smoking ban," Dorothy specifically remembers an early childhood smoking-caused fire in the corn crib. She and her brother, Arthur, had both lit brown-seal cigarettes made from corn fur. She dropped ashes in the corn crib, the barn exploded, and of course, severe punishment followed! However, this was not the first time Dorothy had started a fire. When she was three years old, Dorothy was burned by a pile of leaves. She and Arthur were only supposed to rake the leaves. Because she was "hard-headed," she also lit the leaves on fire. The wind blew some flames on her dress. She began to run and fell in the fire.

If setting fire to the barn and themselves was not enough trouble for Dorothy and her brother, Arthur, to get into when still quite young, playing with a king snake was at least as potentially dangerous. Dorothy tells of seeing one of the huge (probably three foot) speckled king snakes out in their fields while a young child, maybe around seven. She and five-year-old Arthur took off after the snake, hoping to catch it. It dove down in its hole, and trying to play with it, they went after it, too. Fortunately for them, they only got its tail and not its head, that part stayed in the hole. Unknowingly, they were very disappointed that they were unable to extract the snake from his home. Additionally, they were only punished by their mother's wrath for chasing the snake and not the snake's wrath (bite) for also catching it.

"Money does not Matter, only Family"

With eight children in the family, four boys and four girls, it was no wonder the James family struggled. Of those eight children, Carey James was Idora's oldest and first born son. He also was the child she was pregnant with when Joseph James left to serve his country in World War I, in a segregated army, of course. A segregated army where Black soldiers fought among Black soldiers while White soldiers fought among White soldiers even against a common enemy. The segregation of troops was only the theory, though. In reality, segregation was not necessarily a possibility for the actual soldiers, and not completely prevalent, on the battlefronts of France and Germany. In fact, many Black soldiers' journals tell of many Black soldiers who desired to stay in Europe after the battles were won, or at least dreamed of the respect given them by even White comrades, while in the Allied territories. Unfortunately, this same respect was not carried home on the ships with the soldiers coming home. Back in the United States after WWI, the Black soldiers who fought were not considered by many to be any more American citizens than they were before they left. Ironically, Joseph James eventually died from complications caused from fighting the war. He truly died from the poisonous gases he was exposed to in fighting and just plain hard work. Therefore, no one could ever tell any member of the James family that their father was any less an American citizen than any White man.

Carey James was actually born while his father was off to war. Therefore, his father never met this first child until after the War Armistice which was signed on November 11, 1918 at 11:00 a.m. Joseph James was discharged and able to go home after that. Because the baby showed such little family resemblance, the first comment from Joseph upon seeing the baby was, "Is this ours?" Of course, it was. Fortunately, for his progenitors it was, too, because Carey grew up to add twenty-three leaves to the James Family Tree, in single, double, and triple increments.

Shortly after, Bertha, later to become Daniels, was the second born. Bertha still lives in Mississippi and has never driven or had a job, reminding the other siblings the benefits of why they left. Third born was Willie. As already mentioned, Dorothy was fourth. Fifth was Arthur. Sixth was George. These brothers, Willie, Arthur, and George, always were close, in age and temperament, to each other and to Dorothy. Two other sisters followed, Leola and Ruby. Leola, later to be Jackson, also moved west to Wyoming and to this day remains physically and emotionally close to Dorothy. Finally, Ruby, later to be Hills, came as the baby of the family. After two marriages and four children, she lives today in Atlanta, Georgia, although the distance has not separated these sisters in heart.

In essence, Dorothy grew up in a large Black family during the Depression. Because of this, she experienced some of the old-fashioned ideals of that time. Interestingly, when Dorothy was younger, her aunt and her mother would tell the children, when her mother got pregnant, that babies came from trees. So, every Saturday, when her parents went to town to go shopping, she and her siblings would take an axe and a sack to go find trees that had babies in them. These ancient trees were downed, after being dead for decades, if not centuries, so they were easy to chop. However, the children were still terrified that they would cut into the baby's head, and kill the baby, when cutting through the bark to remove the baby. For obvious reasons, they never found a baby in these ancient, dead oaks, though.

To this day, Dorothy questions why her mother and her aunt told her such a far-fetched yarn about where "babies come from" and were so secretive about the "facts of life" with her. Although Dorothy thought it was unfair that her older sister was told the "truth" about babies, Dorothy was glad that Bertha knew about menstruating and the "facts of life" when Dorothy came to that point in her life. When Dorothy was hid in her room, without an ounce of explanation, for two days when "her bleeding started," it was this sister that explained to Dorothy what was going on and eliminated her fears. (Dorothy still has no idea why her mother was more open with one girl than another.) To make matters worse, after that one period at fifteen, Dorothy did not have another for the entire next year. Instead of being open with her daughter this time, again Dorothy's mother was secretive with her. Then, Idora took Dorothy to the doctor to see if she was pregnant, or having any other types of feminine problems, without even talking to her about where they were going, what was going on, or even admitting any of her suspicions. Nothing was found to be wrong, at least as far as Dorothy knew. She was returned home, had periods from her sixteenth year on, and never received any explanation for any of this from her mother even in adulthood. After this, and later experiences in her life that she was not prepared for due to this "protection," Dorothy is adamant to this day about talking openly to her children and grandchildren about all of the "facts of life." She even prides herself on never hiding such "truths" from any family member.

Yes, times and means during the Depression were lean, but like for so many of the rural farmers of that time, Black or White, it did not seem so unusual from any of their previous years of meager existence. "When you did not have much to miss, missing something did not often happen," was a common saying of the time. Some Black people, including the Delany sisters, disagreed, though. Bessie Delanie even stated in Having Our Say that "when times are good for White people, things are tolerable for colored folks. But when times were bad for White people, Blacks were the first ones to suffer… I guess, like anything, it is just perception…There were a lot of rich White men committing suicide, jumping out of buildings and things like that when the Great Depression hit. They must not have had a clue how to live through hard times. Well, the Blacks, and hard working Whites, too, knew what it was to hit bottom, already" (226-227). For the James family, crisis was just a way of life. The Great Depression became just another hardship.

Even during these hard times, the James family had many happy moments. Dorothy still remembers some of those happy times as Christmases as a child. Their gifts may have been very simple: apples, oranges, and dolls for the girls, but "that was okay." The memories were just as good as when the presents may have been more extravagant. They would pop popcorn and string it for decorating the tree. Her mother would also fold newspaper and cut it in a certain shape. Then, the children would use flour and water to mix into a stiff paste and then spread the paste on the newspaper shapes using them to decorate the walls. Another happy time at the James house was

Thanksgiving. For Thanksgiving, her grandparents would come to their home. They did not have turkey every year. At times, they had a chicken that they had raised, instead.

Happy memories did not only have to come with the holidays and special occasions. For Dorothy, like most children of that time, of any color, play did continue to be, even in a minute way, part of their often work-filled existence. All children of "The Thirties" probably played the then popular games of "Ring-Around the Rosie," "Farmer in the Dell," "Who's that Doggie in the Window," and numerous others still played even today. The only difference would have been that Dorothy would have played it on someone else's land, and in general, probably had less free time to play. Specifically, Dorothy remembers fondly the singing of her favorite rhyme: A tisket, a tasket, a green and yellow basket. However, vacations and trips did not exist for Dorothy as a child. Her first vacations nonexistent until after she was married. As children, the James family only went to church and work.

"Grew up Black"

Many games of that day may have been the same for any child, regardless of color. However, color did greatly impact Dorothy's growing up, though, especially as she got older. It first began as little irregularities in treatment. Then, it lead to questions. Later, it became downright discrimination, and finally, created situations that affected her total existence. No wonder Dorothy would often ask her mother from a very young age why things were the way they were. "Why," she would say, "we all bleed the same color?"

Dorothy's childhood questions just went to prove the old saying, "Only little children and old folks tell the truth." After, Idora would then have to answer her daughter that the truth (facts) about "inward color," was "just not the way, because of Southern racism." Outward coloring, no matter how unrealistic it was, did define racial status in Centerville, Mississippi. Simply stated, at that time, and maybe even so today, Blacks and Whites were not treated as equals particularly in the Southern United States. As an example of this, Dorothy recalls the following about this unequal, but accepted class distinction, which was part of her growing up: As a small child, Dorothy, and another small White girl of the same, or even near, age would not be even addressed in the same way. The White girl, even as a peer, acquaintance or "friend," would always be Miss Whatever, when Dorothy would address her, but Dorothy was always, simply, Dorothy. This came to fruition in Dorothy's childhood. While her mother would clean for the White woman, Blanche, and Blanche worked at the Centerville court house, Dorothy, as a very small girl would come and play with Blanche's daughter. Because Emaza was White and Dorothy was Black, even though both were the same age and "friends," Dorothy always had to call the girl Miss Emaza while the girl would address Dorothy as just that.

Not only was the informal addressing of a Black person accepted and condoned, but downright patronizing acts, such as rubbing Black children on the head for good luck, just like a rabbit's foot, were accepted and frequently done. (Speaking of heads and hair, Black and White hairdressers, then and now, joke about the obvious difference there. "It is funny how Black ladies would run out and get their hair *straightened,* and all these White ladies would run out and get their hair *curled.*") All in all, when continually questioned about this, Mother would simply reply, "Dorothy you ask why more than you should, maybe you are too smart and want too much knowledge for your own good, or maybe you are just too Navajo."

Obviously, situations in her early life like this, gave Dorothy reasons to continue questioning the society in which she lived. At one point, she even questioned the "shade issue" among Blacks, themselves. She wondered why different shades of Black people, particularly lighter shades of black, were held in overall higher esteem than the others. (This seemed even more peculiar due to race mixing which made colorings so difficult to even distinguish at times.) This question rose higher in Dorothy's mind as she started learning the "birds and the bees," especially when confronted with an aunt having "white kids" and preferring to have her children look that way. Later, it became evident that it was because the White people would treat her children as lighter-skinned Black people better than darker-skinned Black people. In fact, if they were very light-skinned, Black people were not even treated Black, if no one could tell for sure. However, it would instantly change if they were recognized to be a truly "Black" person. If someone was very dark-skinned, they would be looked down upon, even by other Black people. Many Black people would even treat these lighter-skinned Blacks better than their darker-skinned counterparts. Dorothy, being more "middle-skinned," neither very light nor very dark, only saw the better treatment of the aforementioned "white kids." Therefore, to this day, Dorothy was never satisfied with those "it's just the way" answers. She did learn, however, as another old saying goes, that "if you can't change the world, you can always change yourself, at least on the inside. Then, maybe in the process, "you can change the world just a little."

In fact, this questioning continued, and just escalated, as Dorothy went to school, especially as the family tried to work within the Southern education system, as unfair as it may be. However, they, Dorothy and her siblings, learned early from their mother that education was essential to improving this system. Specifically, reading and writing are the "doors to the world," and make all the difference. Even if the Whites didn't want them to, or did not care if they did, the Blacks learned. The James children went to school, and all including Dorothy, learned to read and write, in spite of these oppressive Southern views. Dorothy liked school, especially spelling and reading. In fact, as a child, Dorothy was the family Book Worm. When Mother taught that "Reading will get you anywhere," Dorothy adhered faithfully to that philosophy. She did not like math, nor do as well in it, as those other subjects. Eventually, Dorothy completed eleventh grade in high school, basically graduating. Around twelfth grade, she met James Hayes, was later able to get off the plantation, and "all was well." Because of this, Dorothy learned that, even with no college education, life was better for her, being educated.

To this day, Dorothy is reminded of going to school and doing her homework whenever she sees, and cleans, Ann Smith's round, oak table here in Cheyenne, Wyoming.

It reminds her of the large round table that her family had in Centerville, Mississippi. Her dad had made it, and it sat in the center of the family kitchen for years. All the James children used this table to do their homework around. At homework time, the James kitchen table almost functioned as a one-room school house; all students working together side-by- side, but each doing their own separate assignments: one would be doing math, another doing writing, and so on. Many times, Mother offered twenty-five cents (a quarter) to whoever finished their studies first. Dorothy earned the money numerous times, but honestly never got the payment. "Times were just too tight to give money away, but they were also very good," was Dorothy's only response when questioned about her Mother's "trick."

Also, education helped the Blacks to cross "a language barrier," since education and language are so closely intertwined; another reason education became absolutely essential to upward mobility. Speech was, and still is, used as a discrimination tool. Black pet names, or terms of endearment such as "love" or "sweetie," so often used by, then and now, Southern Blacks, not excluding Dorothy, were to be used only at home and with other Blacks or very intimate friends. This way, nothing could be misinterpreted. Speech was especially monitored around Whites, so nothing was misconstrued. Dorothy, to this day, uses very controlled speech because of these boundaries. (In fact, I consider it a term of great endearment for Dorothy to call me, "love.") For these same reasons, Dorothy's pet cuss word was then, and is, still the mild 'shoot.' Although the common Black expression "Lordy," or various forms of it, was, and is, not offensive since the term was one of familiarity, and of help, from the Supreme Being, not one of disgrace. This discrimination against speech can be seen in the following example. At a time when it was considered unacceptable to not hire someone because of color; prejudiced employers would still say it was okay not to hire someone due to his or her dialect. In other words, when someone moved particularly into the North or West, he or she could possibility not be hired because they had a Southern accent. It is interesting to note that Dorothy hid her Southern Black accent when she moved West, and very little of it, except these "pet terms" remain, today.

Because of the need for education in Black society, teachers were, and continue to be, an integral part of this society. "Teachers made up the backbone of black middle class, and were, along with the minister, the most important source of black leadership," stated Adam Fairclough on p. 9 of the book, <u>A Class of Your Own: Black Teachers in the Segregated South</u>. These teachers, along with aforementioned minister, shared a belief that education would "liberate the black masses from ignorance, degradation, and poverty" Fairclough added. They insisted that the colored race would "sink or swim" according to the education they received. Therefore, they taught not only the Three R's: reading, 'riting, and 'rithmetic; but such common-sense knowledge as nutrition and cleanliness. Additionally, Blacks learned that to succeed at something they had "not to be just as good, but better at" what they did than any of their white competition, and then never be smug about being better. All of this holds true to Dorothy's education experience, as well.

During her school years, Dorothy's favorite teacher was a traditional Black woman teacher, Ms. Lizzie Jackson. (Nearly 100% teachers of Black children were Black, themselves, and 86% of those Black teachers were also women at the time.) Dorothy greatly admired Miss Jackson for many reasons, particularly the important ideals of common-sense and "being the best." In fact, this fourth grade teacher, Ms. Lizzie, as Dorothy called her, was the person Dorothy listed as the person she admired most from her childhood. One of the first things that Ms. Lizzie taught

Dorothy was, "The best teacher is what you learn for yourself." Second, Dorothy learned of cleaning and organizing from Ms. Jackson. Today, she still holds the teacher's belief that a "housekeeper can always be told from her windows," obviously, the belief of a meticulous cleaner. To be a thorough cleaner is, and was, a life-changing lesson Ms. Lizzie taught Dorothy. This lesson also combated a common belief of the time, and even today, that Blacks are dirty, lazy people that are just not as clean as Whites. Ironically, Ms. Lizzie also used the following phrase, in reference to tidiness: "Cleanliness is next to godliness." This philosophy, in and of itself, should rebuttal another great Black myth, of the "soulless" Black. This myth is especially unfair when so many Blacks, particularly Dorothy, actually base much of their whole existence on their faith in God. Partly because of Ms. Lizzie, Dorothy, to this day spends much of her time cleaning, and not just at work, but at her house, and may well have the "spiffiest-looking yard in her neighborhood." Last, but not least, Dorothy also learned of speech and presentation from Ms. Lizzie. Because of this, Dorothy became a very vivacious student. When Dorothy was fourteen years of age, she was asked to give the daily School Welcome Address. Interestingly, to this day, Dorothy now gives the Welcome Address at certain church functions and services.

It is obvious that Dorothy's family agreed with the Booker T. Washington ideal that the way to improve their race was through education and economics, not political agitation. Still, she questioned why there were both White and Black schools, particularly that there was so much disparagement between the two entities. White schools were cleaner, newer, bigger, and just plain nicer built and better taken care of. On the other hand, Black schools were more run-down, older, smaller, many of which were built with only wood or tin, and often not even schools to begin with. That was the outside. The inside was just as bad, if not worse. The desks, tables, chairs, and other furnishings were often hand-me-downs from the White schools when the White children either got new furnishings or equipment because the old was too run-down for use in their classrooms. The difference in supplies was even more glaring. Books, in particular, were shabby in the Black schools, if the books existed at all. Many times the only books the Black children had to read were the Bible and books from their churches. If they had textbooks or Readers, many of those copies were decades out of date, in raunchy condition, with numerous owners' names written and crossed out from the covers of these books. Even school attendance requirements were different for the Black and White children. Black children were only able to attend a half day of school. They had to spend the other half of the day working on the Plantation (Fairclough).

"Just don't know what Tomorrow Brings"

Schooling was not the only part of life for a Black child that was different than for a White child. All Black people, adults and children alike, were also treated differently in all aspects of the community. Dorothy was no exception. All Blacks, Dorothy included, were only allowed to use separate and segregated facilities in public buildings, sit in the back of public transportation, and enter through back doors. This was in the facilities that they were allowed in. In many private businesses, usually the White owned ones, they were not welcomed at all, and if they were, it was definitely to frequent it in a Black-only section, usually being in the rear. For example, Black community members can only eat at "Black" restaurants. If they ate at "Mixed" restaurants, for both Blacks and Whites, the Black patrons were only allowed to enter through the back door.

Just like the history books teach, Blacks not only entered through back doors, used separate facilities of all sorts, including bathrooms, and were waited on in different parts of restaurants and stores, they also had to sit in the balcony of any type of theater. In spite of this segregation, many Blacks still enjoyed going to the movies. Dorothy was no different. She had always wanted to go to the movies, too. However, due to a lack of funds, Dorothy was not able to attend her first movie until she was fifteen years old. She was first invited to a Joe Louis film; the name has long been forgotten. She was invited to go with her friend, LaCresha, who, unknown to Dorothy at the time, would become her future sister-in-law, a mother to eleven children, and just like her sister Leola, a grandmother to "umpteen grandkids." When it came time to actually watch the movie, Dorothy's experience at the theater was not as pleasant as she had anticipated. When the lights were turned off, leaving the balcony dimly lit, Dorothy was terrified. Sitting in this near-darkness was such a new, never-known-before, sensation for this young, naive teen that she did not know what to do but to hide lying on the floor, quivering. No wonder she does not remember the name of the movie. She did not even see enough of the movie to even know its plot. Her friends must have forgiven her actions at the movies, but not forgotten her, over the years, though. Today, there are four Dorothys, named after our Dorothy, coming from these aforementioned family lines, all associated with those girls at the movies. Interestingly, Dorothy did not get over the "movie-going trauma" easily. She did not go back to the movies until years later when she was in California and went to the movies with her husband. However, she did not have to sit in the balcony at the movies in California. Segregation was just not as prevalent outside the South.

"Segregation had all begun with Jim Crow laws that entrenched in Southern society after 1896, with the Supreme Court ruling in the *Plessy v. Ferguson* case. The case stemmed from an incident in which a Louisiana citizen named Homer Plessy was arrested for refusing to sit in a 'colored' railroad car. Mr. Plessy lost on his appeal to the Supreme Court, which sanctioned the establishment of 'separate but equal' facilities for black and whites. There had been segregation by custom before, but the Jim Crow laws, named for a minstrel show character, made it legal and official... Under the new laws, black Americans faced separate—and inferior—facilities in every part of society, including schools, public transportation, and hospitals. Even public restrooms and drinking fountains in the South were labeled 'Colored' and 'Whites only.' By 1914 every state in the South had passed laws that, in effect, relegated Negroes to a lower status than whites... It would be decades before Jim Crow would begin to finally unravel and that was years after Dorothy left the South... In 1954 the Supreme Court ruled in *Brown v. Board of Education of Topeka, Kansas*, that segregation in the public schools was unconstitutional and the passage of final death knells for Jim Crow" (Gorton 321-393).

Even after Jim Crow days, or in parts of the country where Jim Crow did not officially reign, separation of the races still had a hold on the Blacks through economics. Jim Crow still held onto people's hearts even after it was not the law. Only the South may have prevented voting and running for office by poll taxes, charging money to do these tasks, but Dorothy was taught that everywhere had a pecking order, obviously devised by money status, and as follows: 1-white man, 2-white woman, 3-black man, 4-black woman. Obviously, being both a woman and black affected "pecking order." Though, being black always seemed the bigger issue. Although, sayings today infer pecking order has somewhat changed and hopefully improved. At least in some circles, there are those who are now saying that an older Black Woman has jumped to Number Two, past White woman and Black men.

Therefore, it became economics that truly placed these races and peoples in the aforementioned pecking order. Economics, particularly within family, could not be so easily faked as race and appearance, although it was usually the Whites that had more money, owned the land and businesses, often putting the Blacks down once again. The Black middle class came into being, not because of Whites support, but in spite of it. The Black middle class came to be because of the Black merchants. All in all, Blacks had Black businesses and the Blacks went to these Black businesses. As Blacks improved, they also must watch the fine line between self-improvement through education and education, without threatening and causing intimidation to the White supremacists. Culturally, it has already been shown that Blacks must do tasks at a more competent level than Whites to even be acknowledged. Thus, the Blacks, not the Whites, tried to help their own cross these economic boundary and education boundaries (Gorton 311-320).

However, the real problem came when a Black actually did something out of the ordinary, causing the Whites any type of intimidation. For example, in mixed settings, colleges or the like, the Blacks always earned lower grades. In fact, any possible competition, particularly in education or economics, even could lead further to any number of possible repercussions. Blacks were often wrongfully accused of crimes they did not commit, just like in the play "To Kill a Mockingbird." In the worse possible case scenario, even legal jailings, secret mobbings, complete with possibly deadly lynchings, could be the possible ending. Anything a black said, or did, that a White disagreed with, was open to ridicule, or even punishment. Blacks were often unfairly disciplined, if not "lawed," by the societal rules of the era. Remember, the law, the courts, and the government, were all under White control at the time, and these were the legal systems. No one needs to even mention the implications added by the non-legal, secret systems of control (Lee).

The KKK (Ku Klux Klan) was truly a source of legitimate terror to Blacks. Even today, the KKK makes people, Black or White, shudder because of their secret, violent actions, particularly those of illegal violence, enforcing White dominion using tactics often involving made-up and extreme boundaries. Dorothy's own family was affected by these hidden, racially violence acts. If it was, or was not, the KKK for sure, no one can do anything but guess. By whatever means, Dorothy's own mother, Idora, had both her single brother and two nieces involved in cruel and unexplained deaths. No one was even allowed to investigate, and prove the cause of death, let alone who the perpetrators were. All that is known is that Idora's only brother, Carey, went out one evening after dark to do some kind of work and never came back. That "disappearance" was before 1918 when Idora's oldest son was born and named after his covertly murdered uncle. Years later, Idora's only sister, who also had eight children all of which are gone now, also "lost" her two youngest daughters for no known cause. They were just found in the car, together and dead. The family could not even investigate the scene or study the wounds. They were to take the bodies' home and bury them, no questions asked. So, for years, even today, the questions only can "live within" the hearts and minds of those left behind. Mourning even became overshadowed by the "whys of life" never to be answered, at least in this world.

"Always Runnin'"

At this same time, there were some Northern Blacks, and even some Whites trying to combat the "awfulness" occurring in the South. Progressive Blacks in the Northern cities struggled to change society, specifically through educational and economical methods, particularly for Blacks in cities such as Harlem with strong Black populations. One way Blacks tried to combat discrimination was through the creation of the NAACP (National Association for the Advancement of Colored Persons). The NAACP did, and still does, many great tasks for the advancement of all Americans, especially Black and minority Americans, particularly in the areas of educating and improving life-style, economically and politically, for underprivileged groups of people.

However, in spite of the creation and work of the NAACP, many of the people of the South, particularly the rural south, continued to live in a society where these changes were not even visible. Because of this, country children such a Dorothy, in the 1920s and 1930s, never reaped the benefits from any of the progress gained in that generation. Dorothy still had to walk to school, thirteen miles each way every day. This was because the busses were reserved for white kids. In fact, because of the distance required in walking, and the length of time it took to walk, the White children's bus would almost daily pass the walking James children on their way to school. The bus never passed the James children coming home, though. Black children could only attend a half day of school each day. They must, instead, finish their required farm chores, not attend school, into the afternoon.

The roads the James children walked on, and the White children's busses drove on, were mostly dirty country roads, so the "walkers" were frequently mud splashed. Then, as the White children on the bus passed the mud-splattered victims on the side of the road, some of the more crude children would call "nigger" out the window. Nigger was then, and is especially now, a near-vulgar term, much worse than the disparaging terms of "jiggaboo, pickaninny, and coon" that was so often also used to describe Blacks, especially children. It was often those burly, pre-teen "White Trash" boys who were the worst children for calling such awful names. These arrogant, pre-teen boys were often those who would shortly grow into "Rebbies." "Rebby" was the shortened term for ex-Rebel and better known for racist, white men. With actions like this as a child, there came no hope for more civilized behaviors from these boys when they became men. In the book, <u>Having Our Say: the Delany Sisters' First 100 Years</u>, Bessie Delany, p. 15, is quoted to say, "If I had a pet buzzard I'd treat him better than the way some White folks have treated me!" On days when she was mud-splashed, jeered at, and taunted by children, I am sure young Dorothy agreed.

Although Dorothy was taught to "shrug off" this nasty attitude and meanness with laughter, downright evil acts are nearly impossible to be actually just "shrugged off." Ironically, at the same time, Dorothy was taught to try to ignore these evil urchins, she was also taught to, not just ignore, but always run from white men. These once evil young boys often grew into evil and threatening grown men. So, running was the common-knowledge action taught to Black girls to be done with White men whenever possible. Also, Black girls were not be out after dark, speak to White men, be alone with White men, and other such precautions. Frequently, these precautions still were not a guaranteed protection. This is reinforced by the previously-mentioned Southern "pecking order." Many Southern Whites of that time still did not even consider Blacks as people. No longer could they be property after the liberation of the Civil War, but now many Whites thought and treated the Blacks more like pet animals than people, some even thinking they had no souls.

All this became very evident to Dorothy early on. At fifteen, she was raped by a White man. This was, unfortunately, at a time in Southern society when a colored woman was not safe. Interestingly, rape was not an uncommon occurrence for Black girls of the South to experience. Only now, Dorothy has learned to "fly like an eagle and come past all this." She even admits to never telling her mother of certain situations. Particularly, Dorothy's mother warned her not to go to a certain elementary school friend's house because of the White property owner's reputation. Her mother never knew, at least in this life, of that man's actual actions toward Dorothy. The then-teenage-innocent Dorothy did not understand until it was too late why she was "this once met by that White man that 'owned' her friend's family." (Later, that school friend became her sister's sister-in-law.) She had never even spoken to this man when he came up to her unsolicited. She was then invited to "come see him." Being so young, she did not comprehend the whys and that "old rats love cheese as well as young ones." Now, in her eighties, Dorothy finally admits that "it is all done, got over it at last."

A White man could do anything to a "colored" woman and they would not get in trouble with the law or in any other way. In fact, many White men thought it was status privilege, if not a fringe benefit of being White, to "have their way" with a Black woman. There was even a saying that "Negro blood brings out beauty." No wonder Dorothy's mother had taught Dorothy to run away from White men. However, did it actually prevent the "more-powerful" Whites, especially men, from doing what they wanted, anyway? (Ironically, with all this said, discriminating Whites always have claimed one of the main reasons for their actions of superiority towards the Blacks was so that the two races did not "interbreed" or "race mix.") Fortunately, for Dorothy, she only had the mental traumas associated with such an event to deal with in the long-term. No other additional, possible complications were evidenced in Dorothy's rape crisis. Many other Black girls also lived with much more lasting physical consequences to deal with besides. As stated before, no wonder, Dorothy had so many unanswered questions. Could anyone really answer questions like that?

Dorothy was also "always runnin'," partly because her feet were her only means of transportation. Few people in the 1930s, especially Blacks in Mississippi, owned cars. Somehow, after years of saving, Dorothy's father was able to save enough money to purchase a used Model T. After years of riding in a horse-drawn wagon to church, the James family was elated to ride in a car, especially their own car, no matter how decrepit it might be. Willie was especially excited to be the driver. (Father did not ever have a driver's license since he could not read or write the driver's test.) However, on the way to church, the car just died. Father, and the older brothers, quickly inspected the car to see if they could repair anything and still not be too late for church. It turned out that the battery was okay, gas tank was not empty, and no amount of cranking changed anything. Therefore, to make it to church somewhat on time, Father walked home and returned to the waiting family with their wagon. They had to finish the ride to church as years before, in the wiggly, bumpy and uncomfortable, not-to- mention horse-drawn, old fashioned wagon, nothing new fangled at all. Later that evening, Dorothy's older brothers, Carey and Willie, had to return to the dead Model T and push it home. The car might have been repaired at a later date, but they never figured out why the car died that day on the way to church.

Because there were so few cars, few Blacks, especially women, ever learned to drive. Because driving was such a luxury, Dorothy, as a Black woman in the South would never completely conquer driving a car even after leaving the South. (Her sister, Bertha, who is still in Mississippi, never drove a car at all.) After her few driving experiences, always in someone else's cars,

Dorothy convinced herself that she might just be too nervous of a person to ever drive.

Surely, the following incident also affected Dorothy's desire, if not ability to drive a car, then or ever. When Dorothy was fifteen years old—still too young to even drive legally—she tried driving anyway. She was trying to drive her boyfriend Tommy's car down his driveway after church. She even admitted that Tommy was partly her boyfriend because he owned this car. While Dorothy was heading down the driveway, instead of slowing down, she sped up. At the end of a long driveway appeared a car out of nowhere and she ended up hitting it head on. Because of such a strong impact, the car (which turned out to have twelve or thirteen people in it) flipped, causing lots of screaming and hollering. Dorothy was so "freaked" by all those people screaming and hollering, plus not knowing completely the legal implications that "hitting and running" entitled, Dorothy deserted the scene of the accident and ran home, making it a "hit and run." She also hoped to get away from the scene quickly enough not be known as the cause of the accident when her mother and father found out about it. Truthfully, at the time, Dorothy was almost more worried about being under-aged, driving illegally, and her parent's punishment for that, than the accident. However, by the time she arrived at home, someone had already told her mother and father about the accident. Because Dorothy, nor her parents, did not know at the time the complete extent of the accident, her mother and father were furious enough just about the driving—now even more so because Dorothy had tried to hide it from them. They punished her harshly for those things. Dorothy took her punishment, but because of the harshness of the first punishment she did not explain to her parents about the other incidents of the car crash: car rolling, people screaming and hollering, a boyfriend's totaled vehicle, and so was allowed to go to evening church.

Later that evening, while Dorothy was at church, her parents were to learn all of the facts about the accident, becoming much angrier, when the police would come to their home. The police might have come with the intent of only trying to talk to Dorothy. However, because she was gone from the scene again, the situation just escalated. The policeman followed her to the church. When the policeman found Dorothy "taking attendance" at the church, he had to announce to her in front of the entire congregation that Dorothy had been in this "massive hit and run" accident. Dorothy was also legally required to appear in court the next day. However, no one said to Dorothy what the exact charges were, or any more than there had been injuries in the accident she had been involved in. Not knowing for sure what the charges might be, Dorothy was scared to death to go to court the next day. However, Mother saw that Dorothy got to court the following morning. When all was said and done, Dorothy learned that in actuality two, of the twelve, people in the car had been sent to the hospital, and one lady had a broken collar bone. Fortunately, no one had been killed. Dorothy still wonders to this day what legal consequences would have followed a charge of manslaughter.

Needless to say, Dorothy was traumatized by this car crash experience. However, Tommy was going to save the day. Tommy may have been crippled, bow-legged, and walked with a limp, but he was also quite well-off. Tommy was willing to fix the car if Dorothy would marry him. Dorothy was willing too. However, her mother and father would not give their consent for such a marriage at fifteen. From all this, Dorothy learned that cars were not reasons for boyfriends or marriage.

Even with all this walking, rural Blacks still only owned two pairs of shoes total, one for daily wear, including for school, and one for Sunday wear. To prevent too much wear on the school shoes, much of Dorothy's walking was done barefooted. She carried her shoes to school and church, went barefooted when at play, and had no shoes when the old ones were worn out. She was only given shoes once a year, and when those shoes were worn out, new ones were only purchased the next fall with harvest money. If the shoes were out-grown before fall, the children had to wear them too small, or be barefooted until the next fall. Dorothy's mother even mended old shoes for longer survival, patching holes from wear.

Dorothy's next-youngest brother especially knew of shoe mending. He had some kind of unidentified "potty problems" which made him "pee" everywhere, including on his shoes. Because of the "water" damage and odor, Arthur would often have to have his shoes repaired; cut apart, patched, and re-sewn. Never was buying a new pair of shoes the option. As previously-stated, shoe-buying happened once a year at the most. When buying shoes, usually for the older children, since the younger children always got hand-me-downs, they had to have crop-money. Then, while shopping, they most often frequented Black businesses, so they did not have to sit in the back portion of the White store. Also, in the White store, one had better try on the right-sized pair of shoes because often the shoes, or any other article of clothing a Black tried on, were the one the customer bought. Whites often would not later try on the same clothing a Black had already worn.

"Too Old to Vote"

The Depression was ending with the 1930s, but America only completely recovered economically from it with World War II (WWII). With the manufacturing boom caused by the war that all Americans, Black or White, were once again employed without the help of the Federal works projects. With the bombing of Pearl Harbor on December 7, 1941, the war instead became the national work project. This also brought the war effort, including patriotic renewal, to all within Dorothy's family. After the United

States declared war on both Germany and Japan, three of Dorothy's brothers joined the military to fight in one or the other of these fronts. Although all three men felt some loyalty to this country, they also went to war to get out of Mississippi as soon as possible in one of the few ways possible to do it. Even for those who did not fight overseas in the war, WWII changed life somewhat for everyone. There were shortages and rationings of many commodities, particularly gasoline and sugar. However, for Dorothy, still living on the plantation, times mostly seemed the same, a continued hard life with limited supplies. Similar to the Depression with its shortages and rationings, for those without, these sacrifices seemed much less than for those who had excess. Additionally, since Dorothy did not drive, her feet continued to be her only option, with or without rations on gasoline.

Of Dorothy's brothers, only Carey did not fight in the War. Many joked and still joke that the reason Carey did not join his three brothers in battle was for birth control in the military. Carey eventually had twenty-three children total, and many agreed crudity aside, that he did not need more posterity outside of the States than already would be in the States! Truthfully, he was not accepted into the military because he could not read or write. Brother Willie would come back from the war never to be the same, poisoned with gas. This gassing would be what he would evidentially die from. Youngest Brother George was in the Navy. He came home healthy and only recently died about four years ago. He was living in Las Vegas, Nevada at the time.

During World War II, Dorothy was still a girl and living on the plantation. She had the specific duty of going to the mailbox to retrieve letters from her three brothers in the War. While on this daily task, she met her future husband, James. Dorothy was sixteen years old at the time. James was also young at the time and still living on his nearby plantation, too. James had been born in New Orleans, and moved to Centerville, Mississippi as a boy. Dorothy and James were both basically raised on the same land. Their two plantations were only separated by a barbed wire fence and the acreage of the two plantations.

Even with this close proximity, Dorothy and James did not meet until they were both teens. In fact, at the time Dorothy and James met, James and his father were the only Hayes family members still on the plantation. The rest of the Hayes family had officially left their plantation to "seek their future" in California, away from Mississippi. His family was just tired of the whole plantation/sharecropper thing. James and his father only remained on the plantation trying to "close up its affairs." The only reason Dorothy met James at all, as mentioned before, was because of her checking the mail for letters from her brothers that were "off to war." James was not able to go to the war because of his illiteracy, just like Carey, Dorothy's oldest brother.

He would eventually learn to print his name and not just write an X. When James had gone to sign up for the War, the military would not accept him because of this X. In spite of his writing illiteracy, James always had a good head for "figures" and did exceptional math in his head. As an adult, James learned to print. Also, as a father and grandfather, James tried to learn manuscript because his children and grandchildren, especially Kathy, tried to teach him. However, pride just got in the way for him to completely succeed in doing that. Until the day he died, James stressed to all, especially his children and grandchildren the importance of an education and having the schooling that he lacked.

Interestingly, it was not only the Hayes family that would become tired of plantation/sharecropper life and leave the plantation behind. Also, after years of sharecropping, Joseph James just could not continue this existence as a sharecropper, especially working for "the cheat" like he had. One Saturday, Joseph told Idora that he was done sharecropping forever. That day, he laid down his farming tools and never took them up again. Times had changed slightly from the days of slavery. "Choice-and-say" was becoming an option even in the South. Blacks might have life more difficult than Whites in the South during the 1940s and 1950s, but now they could choose to leave it. Through the following years, Joseph James might have worked just as hard, if not more so, at his new profession. However, this profession was his choice. Specifically, Joseph now worked with puffed wood at the community pulp plant. He only quit working at the pulp mill when he became too sick to work at all. Years later, Blacks would even have a "true say" in the South, "through the vote." Thus came Dorothy's saying "Never too old to vote, until…"

Without that official vote, the Armed Forces were not desegregated until 1948. Therefore, all Black soldiers fought in the Second World War, just as they did in the First World War, as a "separate but equal" fighting force as in all American Wars before, at least the ones they were allowed to fight in at all. The Civil War was the first war Black soldiers were even allowed into combat instead of just doing manual labor. No wonder Mohammad Ali is quoted as saying that there is "No country for the Black American." After being brought to the United States not by will, but by force, Blacks were never even given full citizenship, even in battle, until after this time and with much struggle. Ironically, Dorothy does not know her family's African lineage, and has never even traveled to that continent. Only her nephew has traveled to Africa, and he did not return.

Interestingly, fourth brother, Arthur fought in both World War II and in Vietnam. It was in Vietnam where he lost four ribs. Arthur is still alive today. He is the only one of Dorothy's brothers still living, and currently lives in

Houston, Texas. Unlike the Second World War, the Vietnam War was a much different war for Arthur and all other soldiers, Black or White, to fight in. As mentioned above, Vietnam veterans fought in a desegregated army. However, the war itself was much less successful. In fact, many historians say it was just "one big mistake." Unfortunately, the politicians, have to this day, never even apologized for the debacle we call Vietnam. One of the worst results of the Vietnam War for many Blacks was that it caused a slow down, if not a stop, to the civil rights movement of the time. Fortunately, Dorothy had moved west by then, so her personal civil rights movement seemed to come sooner than for the Southern Blacks. It came in the form of Cheyenne, Wyoming—not a racial utopia by any means, but a much more accepting place than even California, and especially Mississippi.

"Gotta Keep Going"

Whether he, or Dorothy, was in Wyoming, California, or Mississippi, "no other man could step up in my shoes to James Granger Hayes," Dorothy would always say. Who is James Hayes, most people may ask, but not Dorothy or anyone who knows and loves her. James Granger Hayes, nicknamed Brother, was Dorothy's husband of more than fifty years. Because of the difficult life James also led, he would add the following to Dorothy's above-saying: "To wear my shoes, or even my belt, you got to be a man to do it."

James and Dorothy were married January 13, 1947, in Tijuana, Mexico. (James and Dorothy had moved to California in the hopes of work and a better life out West.) The wedding took place in the court house, just down the street from a divorce hall (divorce attorney's office). After a quick ceremony performed by a Justice of the Peace, Dorothy could honestly say, just like in one of her favorite movies, The Color Purple, "I'z married now." Also, once the marriage was all said and done, James's Uncle Bob, who had just paid for the wedding, teased by pointing at the aforementioned divorce hall and asked, "Want that one, instead?" Then, he added, "It would have been cheaper." However, all knew this was a joke because divorce was not common "back then" and not a Hayes family option even now. Once Uncle Bob had paid for the wedding, he also bought dinner and drinks—Tequila—for the in-laws.

Now, about Dorothy and Tequila, there are two isolated incidents involving her drinking, and both times are stories in-and-of themselves. First, there was the wedding. As already mentioned, Uncle Bob not only paid for Dorothy and James's wedding but also the dinner and drinks—Tequila—to celebrate. Of course, Dorothy wanted to join in the celebration. It was her wedding day, after all. However, she did not really celebrate all that much. She spent most of the evening, in the restroom, sick. Because the restaurant had water leaking all the way from the bathroom to the eating area, it made the trip back and forth even more interesting. The posts on the ends of the booths even looked like buoys saying: "Yield for Dorothy, she's sick."

The other time Dorothy drank, and was drunk, was much earlier in her life, but no more pleasant. (No wonder, Dorothy was never a real drinker.) The following helps explain why: During Prohibition, the only drinking that was actually stopped was legal drinking. Illegal brews were "stilled" on farms, in back woods, and for "Speakeasies" in the cities. In Centerville, Mississippi, Icebox Ike was famous in his own right for making his own special "homebrew." Icebox Ike delivered the ice for the local community iceboxes, thus the nickname and permanent access to cold liquor. Dorothy's older brother, Willie, was leaving to go work in the CCC (Civilian Conservation Corps) during the 1930s. The CCC did many government projects, such as building roads and bridges, to give unemployed men work during the Depression. Because Willie wanted to celebrate finding work and to spend time together before leaving with his closest younger sister, Dorothy, they both got some "drink" from Icebox Ike to celebrate. Again, Dorothy only celebrated by "spewing." Although they were wise enough not to drink in the house, Mother still found out. She was irate! Dorothy had to crawl home followed by a flying belt and a bellowing tirade.

Through marriage, Dorothy left school, family, and Mississippi with James. Eventually, because of the Union Pacific Railroad, neither of them would ever go back to Mississippi to live. In fact, Dorothy has only been back to Mississippi twice, once being just last year for a family reunion since her mother died here in 1983. Instead, Dorothy, James, and many of their relatives were, or have become true Westerners. Dorothy and James would first move to California, and later "move on" to Wyoming where they were to settle permanently, making Cheyenne where Dorothy continues to live today with many of her family also here.

"Gotta Survive"

From 1947-1951, Dorothy and James lived in the new world of Pasadena, California. James cooked for his uncle until this man died. Then, he later worked construction. Dorothy, to become James's "Dot" after their marriage, loved the weather and plants of California. She especially loved the fruit anyone could buy there—oranges and such—for next to nothing. Plus, she loved the plants and flowers of California, even the strange ones no one else had, such as palm trees and the like. There must have been hundreds of these strange-looking, beautiful plants growing everywhere. At that time, in California, even poinsettias grew like weeds. Although like many others, it was strange for Dorothy to have to worry about earthquakes. Just to think about the ground moving under her feet, and no guarantee that her own two feet would always be planted on the ground, was a little intimidating.

California weather and foliage were definitely a unique change from Mississippi for the newly-wed Hayes couple, but so were the California people. On a positive note, most Californians were of sunny-dispositions, maybe because of such a temperate climate. The people of California definitely were also more open to all kinds. However, it still was the 1940s, and California's Black (minority) population was still much smaller than it is today. It was in California that Dorothy first encountered many new kinds of people, herself. Dorothy specifically remembers riding her bus home from work with a load of what they then called the "deaf and dumb." Before that time she had rarely, if ever before, associated with the handicapped. Interestingly, both groups used public transportation because neither could drive. Additionally, neither person(s) criticized or ridiculed the other. Maybe all kinds of people, especially the non-oppressed, should study the meaning of this acceptance factor.

While in California, Dorothy had various jobs. First, she worked in the laundry at the Ravenwood Hotel. This hotel was located on the road to Hollywood, now known as Sunset Boulevard. While working at the Ravenwood Hotel, Dorothy had an enlightening discussion with one of the other support staff, a painter. Dorothy was taking a break, peering, probably quite longingly at the hotel guests, as they ran in and out of the building, to and fro from the pool. The painter noticed her thoughtful stare. "They are not happy. They are just passing time," his quiet comment reminded her. His wisdom hit Dorothy like a "ton of bricks." At that day at that time, she truly learned to appreciate that money did not buy happiness. "It just bought more leisure time." Soon after, the conversation ended with a blatant "no" to Dorothy's closing comments of "Do you think we will even get there?" Dorothy confesses that the "NO" has indeed become fact for her. However, from this experience, Dorothy also learned that it did not truly matter. Her life of hard work was just as good, if not better, after all.

In later California years, Dorothy also started cleaning White people's homes. Times were so tough for the Hayes couple while in California, Dorothy was willing to work doing about anything, including cleaning for White people. Some Black people claimed then, and still do, that working for Whites is degrading. Dorothy disagrees: "All the White people I have worked for over the years, even the 'stranger ones,' have been good to me." Plus, Dorothy knew she must do some kind of work just to survive. The newly-married couple had come to California with nothing more than the clothes that they owned. Fortunately, thanks to her mother, to Ms. Lizzie Jackson, and to others,

Dorothy knew how to clean, work hard, and labor for others. Therefore, Dorothy easily got and kept work.

One of the more interesting characters Dorothy has ever worked for was in the Los Angeles area of California. This character was a Millionaire's daughter, and Dorothy again learned that money does not buy happiness, let alone even a good life. This woman, named Eve, but called May, definitely was wealthy, and subsequently, stylish, showing this style in the clothes, particularly in the gloves, she always wore, and in her constant coming-and- goings. However, it turned out that the real reason she was always coming and going was neither wealth nor style. She did drugs, plus dealing and selling to her friends and acquaintances in the vicinity. In one particular incident, and from one particular overdose, Dorothy actually saved her life. That morning, Dorothy overheard this same Eve, who was still in bed, telling her husband, J.B., over the phone, "I won't be here when you get home later this evening." The police were summoned. While there, the police informed Dorothy that she had saved her employer's life. The police added that now Dorothy had the responsibility to prevent the possibility of such an occurrence from happening again. To do this, Dorothy would have to take any narcotics from the medicine cupboard and flush the pills down the commode. Instead of doing any such thing, Dorothy wanted to leave the premises right then and never return. In actuality, she was told she was unable to do such a thing. If she left, she would then become a drug dealer's accomplice. In leaving, she would also take away any protection from this woman's children. So, Dorothy stayed for as long as was possible.

However, after another terrifying experience with Eve involving her Ranch in Palm Springs, Dorothy chose that it was safer to leave than stay. This story goes as follows: Dorothy was told she must ride with Eve to her

Ranch in Palm Springs in order to help with the children. Eve was "drugged," again, so she drove the interstate there at horrific speeds. Poor Dorothy was glued to the back seat in between the children, clutching them, and scared half-to-death. All she can say when remembering this death-defying ride is, "Nobody knows the trouble I've seen."

As soon as Eve and her petrified passengers arrived at the Ranch, instead of being left to mind the children, as Dorothy expected, Eve took Dorothy to a Cowboy Club. Eve's husband was left wife-less, and unwillingly, with their children while Dorothy's unsuspecting new husband was unwillingly left with no knowledge of what was, or could be, happening to his not-at- home, and not-heard-from, wife. After that experience, Dorothy knew she must leave this whole situation behind. She said, "I learned that you can't please everyone, you need only to learn to please you."

Another eccentric woman that Dorothy worked for while in California was, interestingly, also named Dorothy. This affluent woman who shared Dorothy's name resided in one of the most extravagant of mansions that our Dorothy had, or has, ever worked in. This mansion was owned by this other Dorothy and her husband, a management person for Studebaker Autos. In fact, this mansion was large enough to require two cleaning maids. Dorothy was considered the upstairs maid and another woman, Mildred, was the downstairs maid. This household even had a cook, Alice. Additionally, all of this household help were required to wear uniforms to work in. (In much later years, when granddaughter, Pernisha, had to wear a uniform to work waitressing at a fancy club while living in Houston, Texas, it reminded Dorothy of her uniform-wearing days.)   Paul, the husband and official head-of-the-household, was actually only home one time, maybe two times, a year leaving the wife, Dorothy, basically alone and "in charge" of everything, including the children. The couple had seven children, but only one was theirs biologically. No one knows why the husband was so rarely at home or if it had anything to do with why they only had the one biological child or not. Dorothy did find this quite a unique phenomenon, though.

Dorothy is quite certain that at least the parents and mansion owners, Dorothy and Paul, have since passed away. (She was never contacted by the children, for sure, though.) The wife, particularly, is most likely dead for she definitely did not care for herself. Specifically, she would be hard pressed to have outlived the many harmful effects of her chain smoking. Little Dorothy, or our maid Dorothy, who is even smaller now from aging and shrinking, only remembers always seeing Big Dorothy, as they called the aristocrat Dorothy, with a cigarette in her hand or mouth. Ironically, Dorothy added to this commentary on health that "almost all of the people she worked for in California are already gone," specifically due to their unhealthy lifestyles. She added that also, due to their careless lifestyles, were all of the in-laws she was pictured with while in California at a celebration dinner in Tijuana, Mexico "already taken," too. Thus, Dorothy commented on how she learned of "the world" in Los Angeles. In Mississippi, there "just had not been time for all this leisure of smoking, drinking, or cuirassing." Mississippi life, instead, had been "just work and more work."

Another of the homes Dorothy cleaned while in California was of the lawyer, Howard. This lawyer's wife was an alcoholic cutting into Dorothy's wages for her drink, causing Dorothy to not get her "full wage." Because of the wife's drinking, Dorothy came to call the woman the "higher than a kite" mom. When Dorothy came to clean, she would always say, "Hi Dorothy. Gotta run…" Then, she would leave. Dorothy is still convinced that this lawyer's wife was always, "gone," both literally and mentally, the entire time she worked in this home. However, it was not until Dorothy had worked for this family for awhile that Dorothy figured out exactly "where she was always going." Only after a time, did she discover that portions of her salary were also disappearing with the wife. All along, she could sense that something was terribly wrong in this family, though. Her first clue came when the second daughter (there were three) could literally "cuss her mother out in public." The second clue came when the mother attended her oldest daughter's reception "stoned." Finally, the most tragic part of this family's whole saga came when this oldest daughter discovered that she was "fixed." The daughter had gone to the OB/GYNs for answers about having babies, because she desired children after her marriage, and instead found out the "sad truth." Her mother had literally, probably in a nonfunctioning state-of-being, or maybe to prevent an unwanted pregnancy when the girl was younger, "done something surgically" to her oldest daughter, so she could not conceive. Dorothy still remembers holding that daughter, in tears, for hours after that discovery. Not long after this discovery, and because Dorothy was not making the fair and decent salary she deserved for the work she was doing, a change in employment became necessary. After quitting, and even today, Dorothy still wonders what happened to this whole family, particularly the youngest and third, "her honey-child," with this tragic family circumstance.

"Life is what you Make It"

At the same time Dorothy was being short-changed financially by the lawyer's family, James lost the construction job he had in California. This left the new Hayes' family income inadequate to support the young couple. There was just not enough money for California rent and even the couple's basic necessities of life. James was unemployed and Dorothy, with an inadequate job herself, was unable to "make ends meet." James had lost his job because the White men came back from the War. There was just not enough work left for all the workers, returning and already home, especially in construction, and more especially for Black men in construction. It has always been harder for Blacks to get and keep work when competing with White men for the identical manual labor jobs. For James to get work, a change was required in the family's living circumstances. This needed change came with a move to another western state. This time the move was to Cheyenne, Wyoming.

Interestingly, just as life was changing, and improving, for the Hayes family out West, "the decades following the end of World War II were an era of new hope for Black America. Under pressure from Congressman Adam Clayton Powell, Jr. and A. Philip Randolph of the brotherhood of Sleeping Car Porters, President Harry Truman desegregated the armed forces in 1948. Several years later, with the Supreme Court's ruling on Brown v. Board of education of Topeka, Kansas, desegregation of schools became the law of the land…Then, on December 1, 1955, a department store tailor named Rosa Parks singlehandedly assailed the Jim Crow laws by not giving up her seat to a white man on a bus in Montgomery, Alabama. Her protest sparked a revolution, spear-headed by the Reverend Martin Luther King Jr.—a decade of protest against racial discrimination at the voting booth, and in school, employment, and public accommodations. Television cameras rolled as white lawmen beat back the protestors with clubs, dogs, and fire hoses. The demonstrators' slogan was, 'the whole world is watching,' and indeed, those images of violence would help secure passage of landmark civil rights legislation guaranteeing Black Americans their full constitution prerogatives…and that offered a lifestyle that had begun to represent the American dream" (Delany 273-274).

The Hayes family's improved living condition specifically came not just because of the physical move from Los Angeles, California area to Cheyenne, Wyoming, but was also because of these civil rights events of the time. These improvements could be specifically seen in the better working conditions of James Sr., coming in the form of a different, and better, job. The job change was due to securing work with the Union Pacific Railroad. This union with the railroad would end up lasting well over thirty years. When Dorothy and James first moved to Cheyenne, they moved into the railroad section of town. They lived in a one bedroom house with a shared kitchen and bathroom for both them and their landlady. While living in Cheyenne the first time, their address was 1811 Thomes Ave.

Dorothy again owed her In-laws for the job in Cheyenne, and with Union Pacific, which were to end only after more than thirty-five years with the U.P. It was with one of these brothers-in-law that Dorothy also so fondly remembers square dancing with. James would not square dance, Dorothy quite liked it, and so she and her brother-in-law would often square dance together. She also enjoyed her work at the nearby bakery. Her first job in Cheyenne was at this neighborhood bakery close to her new home on Thomes. Later, the same ex-Southern girl left the bakery to become a "Hitching Post Salad Girl"—meaning the "fancy" salad chef at that restaurant while her sister, Leola, who had also moved to Cheyenne, was the "Little America Salad Girl." (Ironically, both sisters had always been taught to treat people "with molasses, not vinegar," and now they were making salads for people "with vinegar, not molasses"!)

Leola and Dorothy have always been close sisters, both in spirit and proximity. They became particularly close as adults. "In spirit," the sisters were "specially attached by relationship." Dorothy's childhood friend, LaCresha, became Dorothy's sister-in-law, and Leola's childhood friend, Katy-May, became Leola's sister-in-law. In "living distance," the sisters were never far apart after both moved out West. In fact, they were often physical neighbors. Dorothy lived next door to Leola in the railroad housing at Buford. (James had gotten Leola's husband, David, a railroad job also in Cheyenne area.) In Cheyenne, even today, Leola and Dorothy live only two blocks apart. One of their jobs is even together. With both sisters out West, their mother had suggested that they live close enough together to take care of each other. The sisters followed this suggestion and both were blessed by it.

Although the sisters are so close in spirit and proximity, their age, build, or life experiences may not have always correlated. "Little Leola" as Dorothy calls her sister, who is many years younger, was also physically much smaller than Dorothy until quite recently. Her size changes probably are direct symptoms of the major life difference between Leola and Dorothy. Leola had twelve children, one of which was still born. (However, Dorothy was always okay with only having the four children—two boys and two girls-- that she and James were blessed with.) Leola's husband, David, on the other hand, had fourteen in his family growing up, so hoped and succeeded in having a very large family.

Leola had so many children, and later so many grandchildren and great-grandchildren, that she once admitted to losing count of her posterity. Dorothy has also encountered some unique comments and stories for being Leola's sister and because of all of Leola's children. Once, Dorothy was questioned by a Mrs. Jones at the base if any Black person in Cheyenne was not related to Dorothy. Dorothy had to admit that she only knew for sure that she was not related to anyone on base. Even one of Leola's children asked Dorothy when she was younger: "Aunt Dorothy, are you related to everyone in Cheyenne because of us?" Dorothy teased back that maybe, but she did not think so. However, she added further that she could be related to more of Cheyenne than she thought before because she has now lost count of her great-nieces and nephews. "There always seem to be some new nieces, nephews, and great-nieces and nephews popping out," she joked. She even admits to sometimes having a hard time keeping track of all of Leola's descendents. In fact, at a recent great-nephew's wedding, Dorothy met three new great-nieces and nephews she thought she had never even seen before. One was an Isaiah she was positive she had never met before. She also knew he had to be at least three or four years old. In reality, he was at least old enough to come up to Dorothy on his own, introduce himself to "Aunt Dorothy," and then carry on a complete conversation with her.

Moving to Cheyenne was unique for all of the aforementioned born-and-bred Southern youth. Weather was a particularly interesting change. California may have been more temperate, less humid, and just more agreeable than the Mississippi heat, but Wyoming was just downright different. Where neither Centerville, nor Pasadena, had winter to speak of, Cheyenne definitely did. In fact, the first winter that Dorothy and James spent in Cheyenne, Wyoming, was a record-breaking snow year. The first snow storm Dorothy ever saw, let alone lived through, happened in October 1951. (Before this, Dorothy had never even seen snow.) During this storm, the young couple actually had snow drifting from the ground to over their roof. Dorothy had only known that the weather that day was getting dire because the windows were getting dark from the storm. She did not realize, however, it was the snow covering the windows, not just the clouds covering the sun.

Not only was this first winter, and the weather, an adventure for the "newly-formed" Hayes family coming to Cheyenne, many said the "water" was too. Who knows, maybe it was the water, Dorothy and James had been married eight years with no children, and both were over thirty, but when they came to Cheyenne and tried that Cheyenne water, something changed. James Jr. was born February 7, 1955, and Kathy was born August 5, 1956. James Jr. was only six months old and his mother was pregnant with Kathy. Eventually, the Cheyenne area would be the birthplace for all the Hayes children.

"Little House on the Prairie"

As much as the "weather" and the "water" of the Cheyenne railroad community was a new experience for the Hayes family, moving to the Buford railroad community was not. Not long after James Sr. was assigned to Cheyenne with his job on the railroad, he was reassigned to the rural train sections outside of Cheyenne. Therefore, the small, but growing, Hayes family moved to Buford. Buford was physically only about twenty miles from Cheyenne, but it was miles back in time for living circumstances. Dorothy honestly believed that once she had married and was "out of" Mississippi she would no longer have to deal with that out-dated life style. Instead, the Hayes family lived in Buford, Wyoming for seven long years almost as pioneer settlers would have fifty years before. First, they had an "Outside House," their southern term for our outhouse or modern "porta-potty." Additionally, each Buford family got their water from a pump hydrant also "out-of-doors." Finally, their heat came from coal. This, however, was Dorothy's first experience with coal heat and the retrieving of coal from a coal bin, a messy and difficult task for even an experienced "coal-user." Still, the family quickly became very grateful for the warm, effective coal heating system because of the freezing cold winter weather of Buford. Cheyenne had been bad enough but Buford was nearly unbearable with the wind howling down on their small A-frame "railroad-housing-surplus" house. Worse yet than Cheyenne, Buford was set on the hilltop and was complete with only all those aforementioned outside amenities. It was even possible with such difficult times, (and lonely times because James was often gone on the railroad), with all the hauling and dumping of water and coal, that Dorothy's physical health was compromised. She had no more children in Buford, but two miscarriages. However, the growing children, James Jr. and Kathy, did enjoy their childhood in Buford and attending the almost one-room school house of Willadsen School. These preschool and elementary school years of the first two Hayes children were pleasant with their parents on the Prairie. All of this, nevertheless, did make Kathy feel a little like Laura Ingalls Wilder living in her "Little House on the Prairie."

One of Dorothy's most memorable experiences of living on the Prairie was related to getting Leola from the wilderness to civilization when Dorothy's sister was in labor with one of her seven girls, Georgia. All of the seven girls and five boys of Leola, except this daughter, even when their mother was living on the Prairie, were delivered in the hospital. However, Georgia was born in the car on the way to the hospital. Georgia is still teased that she has a small head because of being born in the car and being dropped on her head during that delivery. Dorothy was especially involved with this baby's delivery because Leola requested Dorothy's specific help with it. Dorothy was out at the Buford Post Office getting her family's mail when Leola called to Dorothy to go get her husband. Leola's husband was out "over-the-hill" working at the train yard. It turned out that Dorothy had enough time to "wash Leola's feet" (an old Black mid-wife comfort technique) before David came in, though. He had stalled in coming, so he could get his work finished at the train yard. Unfortunately, he should not have stalled then because he was to be still more delayed from getting his wife to town after that. This time, it was because he had to fix the motor on their personal "struggle mobile" (vehicle) since it then would not start when David thought it was time to go. After all these delays, Georgia ended up being born in the car.

Later, the Hayes family moved again, still on the Prairie, though. This time it was to Borie, another railroad section with housing. This section was out by Granite and Crystal Reservoirs. Borie was the family home when Brenda was born in the Cheyenne hospital. It was March 9, 1964. Borie was also actually where Willadsen School was, so while the Hayes children lived there they did not have to be "bussed" to school like they had when at Buford. Ironically, Borie may have been nearer to civilization in proximity to Cheyenne, and eventually brought the Hayes family back to Cheyenne, but was not closer than Buford with its enmities. Living at Borie, Dorothy still had to use an outside water pump, to heat the water, and survive an outside house, just like at Buford. The Hayes family never actually lived at the third railroad section, outside of Cheyenne, the Granite Train Section. However, Leola Jackson, Dorothy's sister, with her husband and family, lived at the Granite Train Section while the Hayes lived at Borie. This became the sisters' only, and farthest, separation while both lived out West.

Part II: To Bent Ave

Part II—To Bent Ave.

"Better, not Perfect"

"Step up in the Trail"

"Look down the Road"

"Driving Mrs. Dorothy"

"Step up to the Plate"

"Sewer Rat"

"Grandma Dora"

"Faith: Land versus Water"

"I'm just Nobody Trying to help Somebody"

"Just too Young"

"Keep on Workin'"

"Get Da Steppin!"

"It's a Blessing to Help"

"Never had it to Miss"

"Blood is thicker than Mud"

"Flying like an Eagle"

"I'm not a senior citizen...I'm a recycled teenager."

"Epilogue"

"Better, not Perfect"

With the two children reaching their teen years, a move back to Cheyenne in the middle 1960's was inevitable. This way James Jr. and Kathy could attend junior high school in town since Buford/Borie only had the elementary school. They officially moved back to Cheyenne around 1964-5. Granddaughter, Ashley Rambo, beautifully describes where Dorothy still lives in town, like this: "Somewhere in Wyoming's high plains, amid its brown, dry, and dusty Western atmosphere lays the capital city, Cheyenne. Living in town near the Frontier Days Fair Grounds, in an older, once black-only, suburban neighborhood, shaded by trees is her current and long-time home."

James and Dorothy purchased the house Dorothy now lives in, 2719 Bent, a few years before moving back to Cheyenne, while still in Borie, and rented it out, in anticipation of this eventual, and necessary, move back to

Cheyenne. Ashley described her grandparent's home in the following touching way: "The house consists of four main sections. In the front of the house is the front porch and sun room. This room is made of mostly glass. The room is filled with green life, flowers, and chairs. Fragrant smells of flowers and trees float along the air, and the chairs are there for admirers to sit in and escape. Past the sun room is the living room… I close my eyes and instantly recall the booming voices of my grandpa and loud men where the men usually chat and watch baseball, gathering facts and tips about hunting and fishing. 'Well y'all know I caught myself that ol' sun-a bitch catfish. Got me's the Wyoming record' shouts my grandpa James… and from beyond in the kitchen, along with the gossip-like giggles of the women replies my grandma, 'You's be telling that ol' funky story again James. I says give it a rest' and she calls all the females into the bright, yellow kitchen to help. Finally, from the kitchen is the back porch coming out of the kitchen backdoor leading out into the backyard alive with greenery always grown by Grandma, too." After a home depiction such as this, it is no wonder the kitchen still houses the famous Fisherman's Prayer plaque that says: "Let me catch a big enough fish to tell no lies."

Overall, Cheyenne was a superior place for the Hayes family to live in. It was not the hot, humid, and racist South; the temperate, over-crowded, and new-fangled California; or even the gusting, frigid, and lonely Buford. Although occasional hate crimes occurred in Cheyenne, (crosses in neighbors' lawns and black churches' grounds), these Black people encountered more racial acceptance and a more "normal" existence in Cheyenne than ever before. No longer did they have to be taught why they were, and it was okay to be, different. The Hayes' family was now the average child, teen, or adult members of the Cheyenne community.

"Step up in the Trail"

"You're a man, so step up in the trail." These were the words that Dorothy would often tell her first-born, and delightful-to-know, son. James Jr. replied with the following few words about growing up as a Hayes: "First, my most memorial event as a child was the time when I asked my dad if I could play at Wendy's. She had a trampoline. He said ok but be back before dark. Well, I wasn't and couldn't sit down for a week. I definitely learned that day that 'a hard head makes for a soft behind.' Second, my most memorial event as a teenager was when my father stood up for me to the police and told them to take him for they were wrong about me. Next, when I think about Christmas as a child, I remember they were 'all filled with love.' Finally, when I am asked about my mother I think of when Kathy, my sister, was visiting, and we went to Snowy Range. There we met some people who were tourists, and when they met my mom, they thought she was an angel sent."

Additionally, as a boy, James remembers going to the 4th of July railroad picnics, the special family traditions as a child of hunting—deer and antelope—and fishing trips with the cousins. Of his childhood friends, James' most memorable friend was also a James (James Phillips) known as Bucky, maybe to keep them straight. It was Bucky who gave James his first cigarette at the movies. Of childhood heroes, the person James admired the most was Nelson Mandela.

Last but not least, even though James Jr. answered "nothing" when asked what was special about him, Dorothy's aforementioned request of proven manhood shows everyone that James Jr. is much more valuable than he volunteers. James Jr.'s worth was reiterated when James Sr. would not allow his son's friend, Billy, come over any more. The friends were doing drugs and alcohol together, perpetuating the other in these vices. James Sr. also knew Billy's father was a good man who was Sioux Indian. Because both men wanted something better for their sons, James Jr. accepted this and simply stated, "My dad told his dad not to let me come over anymore. His dad didn't. And that was that!"

After James Jr. moved back to Cheyenne, he attended the old McCormick Junior High and Central High as an average youth there, except he played some exceptional basketball. In fact, he was nicknamed Dr. J by Keith, his younger brother of twelve years. Keith added, without solicitation, how much he looked up to James as his older brother and as an admirable character. This was verified when James Jr. "took the rap" for his cousin and went to Worland from February –September instead of graduating from high school. Why? Basically, some White boys and Black boys were getting "into it" over the weekend, James Jr. went home and got his Dad's gun, the cousin fired the gun at the White boy's car, and James, being the Black boy and the gun owner's son, was punished. However, "all turned out for the best," after James Jr. "took the rap." From there, James Jr. earned his GED, vowed to never have any trouble with the law again, which held true, and went on be a very productive member of society.

James Jr. would later attend junior college for a degree in refrigeration. From there, he has for many years worked, and continues to work, for the Blue Cross maintenance crew. To this day, he happens to still live around the corner from his mom and is often seen helping her out. Currently, his official address is on Thomes with his significant other, Annette, but to see him at Dorothy's house is never a surprise. To sum it all up, James recently had surgery, and all tease that because he is still like a kid about needles, Dorothy again had to remind him, "You're a man, so step up in the trail." Which he did, of course!

"Look down the Road"

It was barely a year when the second born Hayes child, Kathryn (Kathy), arrived. Kathy particularly remembers her childhood as a Hayes for birthdays because '"Mom was great." Being a summer baby, she didn't get to celebrate it at school, so her mother still always made it special. In Kathy's words, "Mom did it up for me, from Buford to Borie to Cheyenne, there was always family, friends and FOOD!"

Kathy also emphasized that her childhood highlight was Christmas. In her own words, she said the following: "Living at Buford was like 'Little House on the Prairie' and so was Borie. But Christmas was Wow!—cutting down our tree, making our own decorations, finding the right tumble weed, stringing popcorn and cranberries, and our Christmas program. When you live thirty miles out of town shopping is something to look forward to. Snow, snow, snow, is what Mom loves—well, now sometimes.

Christmas morning Mom would get us all dressed up, and a bus would pick us up and take us to Cheyenne, arriving at the Plains Hotel, a fabulous place back then. We started with breakfast, then music, games, and socializing with all these different kids whose Fathers and Mothers did the same thing. Then we went to the Paramount Theater to watch cartoons and a Christmas movie, two of them I think. After the movies, we headed back to the Plains Hotel for lunch, and while you were inhaling great food, all of a sudden 'Ho, Ho, Ho, boy ooh boy, Santa Claus.' They treated us so great and safe, and they gave great gifts to our parents too. That is a wonderful family tradition we all looked forward to until they stopped doing it."

Kathy also specifically wrote about the 4th of July and having all of the family over for "Dad's Fabulous Bar-B-Q warm summers, and Mom working the room—greeting, hugging, kissing, shaking hands, smiling, and making you feel so important--Welcome." By this following statement, "watching Mom and Dad get ready for a feast of love, joy, and fun," anyone could easily tell why to this day Kathy still loves the 4th of July. If the 4th of July family gatherings were not pleasant enough memories, Kathy added the UP (Union Pacific) summer picnics as a childhood feast of food and friendship, too. She said, "As long as I can remember, there were really 'cool' events through the UPRR (Union Pacific Railroad) where my father worked for over 38 years. His union, (The Brotherhood of Maintenance of the Way), they would have the best summer picnic with games and fishing, baseball, horseshoes, swimming, and of course food. And Dad always did the Bar-B-Q."

Not only did Kathy fondly remember events, she distinctly remembers people. Her best childhood friend was Nila Marie Flowers who also "lived at Buford." Kathy tells the following of Nila: "We are the same age and we played together every day. We were so close that we would exchange baby bottles. Her mother's name is Helen and her father, Bob. They were the coolest people and the only Irish family at Buford. At my birthday parties it would be Nila, my brother, all my cousins, Bobby, and his brother. Bobby and his brother were from the only Mexican family." How like Dorothy, to have her Black children and Black nieces and nephews invited and associating at her child's birthday party with the only Irish and Mexican family at Buford. Obviously, the child Kathy noticed and grew-up with a positive response to all this as her stated reaction shows only how much she respects and learned from her mother. She even concluded with this affirmation: "Our mothers would say you care; I don't care!"

The teenage Kathy Hayes continued to be and was always a "people-person," a quality frequently admired about her. In fact, her mother would even call her "Miss It." Kathy herself agreed, "I left so many wonderful people behind when I left Cheyenne. I love the saying 'a stranger is a friend you haven't met yet.' I collect people; I like people. They are amazing! When I come home I look some of them up and we pick-up where we left off and continue on. Friends from high school, friends from the health club I worked at, friends I would party with, lots and lots of good loving friends. And they love my mother too."

However, everyone agrees that there are no negative connotations when it comes to Kathy being a socialite. She has and continues to be someone very notable and has been very successful in school, relationships, and later, in life. As a teenager, she even supported the popularity of family over that of friends. Specifically, she said, "I liked hanging out with my parents. I guess this would be shown best by an incident I had after my high school graduation before I was off to college. The first time I got drunk I had just turned 19, drinking age back then. Two friends celebrated with me. Two drinks later, I was back at home with my forehead against the wall. They knocked on the door and left. Mom opened the door and there I was. She helped me in and put me to bed; kept her cool the whole time."

Kathy continues on about the importance of family with "I come from a big family, with that came a lot of people. Being away for so long, I don't have a lot of recent stories to tell. My stories are more from growing up. Then, Mom did always give advice on so many things: life, men, boys, girls, people, and periods. But I would have to say how much I admire about my mother and growing up with her until I got married myself, also became a mother, and moved away. This 'wonderfulness' of my mother was truly shown the day I got married. It was on a Monday and my mother arranged my reception in two or three days. It was lovely! Also, she has so much knowledge. And her spirit and faith are strong. She is so strong. I am so grateful for my faith because my mother gave me a foundation built on faith and hope plus love and humor. My mom can be one funny crazy lady. I thank her so much for all of that."

To this day, Kathy continues to be, according to her brother, Keith, "just as fun and always the social butterfly." In fact, her living is made working with people (Domestic Clienteles) or cleaning house for them just like her mother. In conclusion, Kathy herself finishes by saying that the most special part about me is "How about…I am my mother's daughter. I tell friends, family, acquaintances I want to be like her (Mom) when I grow up. So far…aaa (laugh) I am a better wife, mother, friend, aunt, sister, I hope from my mother. Thank you!"

Kathy would, as she told, marry well and move to Boardwalk Way, Kelso, Washington. Her husband is Scott Rambo whom she met while he was with the Service in Cheyenne. He is a fair amount older than Kathy (Ironically, Scott was married before, to a Kathy, even) but that is okay to all of the Hayes family. They call him "white and wonderful." Dorothy to this day adores her son-in-law and especially now enjoys his pet name of Dossy. With the positive family reaction to this mixed marriage, it is obvious to see the Hayes family as accepting, progressive, and living a tolerant lifestyle in, hopefully, a more tolerant society.

Even though the Rambo's have an interracial marriage (mixed marriage) in a more progressive day and age, Kathy and Scott face many issues common to mixed couples, particularly Black and White couples. One of their biggest people obstacles came from Scott's own father. It took her father-in-law, Gail, the birth of his first, and only granddaughter, and a losing battle with Cancer "to come around and accept, even love" his daughter-in-law, Kathy. Dorothy even promised her daughter if she would always be Christian to her father-in-law he would come to admire her and know she was not "stupid." In this case, truth was validated with "what comes around goes around."

In fact, Gail has come to visit Dorothy and Cheyenne. At this point and time, Gail will now even request Dorothy's baked beans and potato salad, again reiterating the power of, someone like Dorothy, true tolerance, and maybe even food. Ironically, the reconciliation did not occur before James Sr.'s death in 2000. Shirley, Scott's mother, White enough to have dyed orange hair, was much quicker to turn around and even accepted Kathy from the start. Some may say Kathy moves "slower than Christ's coming," and some of the changes in her life have come slowly too, but overall her life proves that change is always "better late than never."

On a positive note, times were starting to change for the better, even racially, all over the United States about this same time that life was also improving for the Hayes family. It must be conceded, though, that the South was still responding at a much slower pace to this racial tolerance than the North and the West. In the mist of this historical upheaval, though, just like in most historical upheavals, most of the people only lived on in their average fashion.

So while the Hayes family was marrying, given in marriage, bearing their children and just living a daily existence, the Civil Rights issues of the day were circling around them. Even in their more racially-accepting home of the time: Wyoming, Civil Rights issues existed. Specifically, "two prominent Wyomingites watched as an African-American serviceman and his spouse seated themselves in the little café at Cheyenne's Plains Hotel in 1954. The couple sipped water and read the menus. Suddenly a waitress jumped from her station and snatched away the menus. The manager entered the scene and ushered the two African-Americans out of the restaurant.

Teno Roncalio and Dr Francis Barrett discussed the shameful incident they had witnessed. An African-American soldier who had probably served his nation during World War II could not eat at a restaurant in his own country. How could an American citizen be so mistreated? Thoughts of such injustice infuriated Roncalio and Barrett. Roncalio, a rising star in the state Democratic Party, and Dr. Barrett, son of Republican U.S. Senator Frank A. Barrett, sought to intercede with the Plains Hotel. The manager explained that he did not dictate hotel policy, but instead followed directives from the Plains' ownership. When Roncalio and Barrett contacted the hotel owner, they obtained no satisfaction. Outraged, attorney Roncalio began to confer with the Wyoming Democratic Party about the problem…However distant Wyoming might have been from the segregated South (the focus of the early post-World War II civil rights movement), the Equality State was hardly immune from discussions of racial justice. Along with several other developments, the incident at the Plains Hotel helped mobilize support within Wyoming for improvement in the treatment of minority citizens" (Ibach and Moore 1).

The following scenarios discuss the true racial climate of Wyoming at the time and are also totally reflective of the Hayes family situation of the time: "World War II proved to be a major watershed for American racial relations. Prior to Pearl Harbor, African-Americans in southern states generally worked as unskilled laborers or sharecroppers. In the North, they took comparable low-income jobs. As American involvement in the war increased, employment opportunities for Black Americans improved. Due to a dramatic labor shortage, African-Americans also found jobs in the West... More than a million southern African-Americans migrated northward and westward during the war, catching the attention of vote-conscious White politicians in the process...Quite self-consciously, and for a variety of reasons, westerners began to participate more fully in discussion of racial equality"(Ibach and Moore 1).

In actuality, the racial issues in Wyoming can more honestly be traced to Wyoming's lack of Black people and exaggerated sense of independence rather than to racial prejudice. "Wyoming's traditional demographics and culture encouraged a sense of distinctiveness on civil rights matters. To begin with, the state was overwhelmingly White. The 1950 census records show Wyoming's total population as 290,529 people, 6,520 of whom were counted in the 'non-white' category. Only 2,557, less than one percent of the total population was labeled as 'Negro.' By 1960, the state's total population increased by 39,537 people, but the African-American numbers actually decreased by 374. Under that same census, the total non-white population grew by some 624 people. Wyomingites also blasted an image of exaggerated independence and individualism—as a people distinct from the rest of

America. Even after World War II, when economics and technological advances (paved roads, more autos, electrical utilities, circulation of newspapers, and radio programs) united rural Wyomingites, the sense of isolation and distinctiveness often persisted" (Ibach and Moore 2-3).

Finally, it was the 1964 federal act against racial discrimination that made the most long-lasting legal changes for Black persons in the United States, particularly in Northern and Western regions of the country including Wyoming. This biracial support came where "at least outside the South, white Americans in large numbers found Martin Luther King, Jr.'s appeal for justice and racial conciliation appealing, even ennobling. The non-violent civil right demonstrations, combined with an often violent or obstructionist White Southern response, made it relatively easy for Americans elsewhere to choose sides. This was especially the case by the late 1950's when the new medium of television broadcast the drama to millions of viewers in the safety of their living rooms. Given the state's small African-American population, Wyomingites of both political parties had little to lose by eliminating the vestiges of school segregation or opening up places of public accommodation to members of all races. As the language of Roncalio, Barlow, and Governor Simpson suggested, support for this kind if civil rights campaign seemed the essence of Americanism. By adopting these proposals, moreover, Wyoming could at least appear to be on pace with states outside the South" (Ibach and Moore 3).

"Driving Mrs. Dorothy"

Partially racially-based, everyone who knows Dorothy knows that she does not drive. One of the main reasons Dorothy does not drive has to do with her growing-up situation in the South, partly of being Black and a woman, and also including the crash Dorothy was involved in as a teenager--a story already told in great detail. However, that was not the only crash Dorothy was involved in. In fact, every story Dorothy tells of herself and of being "behind the wheel of a car" appears to end in a "crash." Another "Dorothy automobile crash" happened when she was pregnant with Brenda and having some early labor pains. She, probably, partly because of the previous miscarriages, became very nervous from these labor pains. Due to her fear, and being alone with the other children, decided to drive to the hospital for help. Instead, she drove into the neighbor's front window. Obviously, she had to give up on the driving to the hospital plan until she could be escorted there by someone else. All turned out to be okay with Brenda when she and James Sr. got to the hospital later, but Dorothy did have to replace the neighbor's window. After these two aforementioned scenarios, Dorothy has not driven since.

Kathy added the following story of Dorothy's driving: "There is another reason why my mother doesn't drive. We were living at Borie, Wyoming: James, Brenda, when a tiny baby, Mom, and I. Mom wanted to go on a picnic and it is summer. So we packed a basket and diaper bag and loaded up into the car. Mom backed out of the driveway all the way until we were hanging over the ledge where below were the railroad tracks. She did pull forward, unload the car, and we all walked to our picnic, instead. After that, we had a great day!"

This stress of driving, and "crashing," cars also did seem, at one point, to carry over from Dorothy to her eldest son. In his "early" driving career, James Jr. "accidently" tried driving the family car but ended up with him and Kathy driving into the "outside house at Buford," instead. James Jr. was only about four years old and playing in the car with Kathy, three. James Jr. knocked the car into gear and headed down the hill. Fortunately for the two children and their mother who saw what was happening and came running from the kitchen after them, the Buford outside house blocked the ravine making the car then "crash into the outside house." More fortunately for all, the car was stopped by the impact from the outside house and did not roll over the cliff. The outside house did have to be rebuilt, however.

"Step up to the Plate"

Therefore, most of Dorothy's life was actually just spent "non-driving' and in day-to-day living. Although it was at the same time as many of the aforementioned political rights battles, the Hayes family usually just continued to fight the day-to-day battles of a young, but growing, American family. In fact, in March of 1964, they welcomed their third child, a second daughter, Brenda. Interestingly, it is Brenda who is to this day a strong political advocate for Black and Women's Rights. In fact, Brenda is currently the Vice President of "Love and Charity," a Cheyenne group for Black women. She was also recently given a picture of Martin Luther King and President Barak Obama from a doctor whom she works for.

These are some of the signs of what kind of a person Brenda is. Dorothy describes her as "such a worker, not just a talker. She is always doing something to help and standing for what is right." She adds that Brenda is a true Christian because she so exemplifies the saying: "Hippocrates run, but Christians stand!"

Dorothy does have to admit that Brenda is "all Hayes, and no James." In fact, she also admits that Brenda was always the one "to step up to the plate and be a woman." Others in the family have added that being a Pisces (a March baby) fits Brenda to "a T." Just like Brenda, a traditional Pisces is compassionate and kind, while yet being idealistic, plus forceful and strong when needed. Therefore, in Brenda's case Dorothy has said that "her Horoscope suits her and is not just silly to read."

One example of Pisces Brenda was when she was a toddler. Because she saw the bus driver's dog just sitting alone, waiting by the bus, she had to go pet it. Instead of the favorable response she expected, she was bitten by the over-protective, and somewhat aggressive animal. The dog had jumped off the bus meeting Brenda and had bitten her before she was even able to actually fully approach the dog herself, or be stopped from approaching the vicious animal by any observing adults. Because Brenda lived in the rural train section of Borie at the time, she had to be brought to the doctor's office in Cheyenne and be stitched up. Yes, Brenda was a truly sympathetic Pisces to show such kindness to a not-so receptive dog.

Pisces Brenda also demonstrated the idealistic and "strong" side of that Zodiac member in the explanation of her character from younger brother Keith. He described her with much admiration as "Brenda is Brenda." She was, and continues to be, his "big sister," literally. Like any older sibling to a younger sibling, Keith also tells of how Brenda did the usual "picking on me." However, he adds the following story of the 6th grade bully. This bully had terrorized a much younger Keith so much that Keith had even vacated the swings for this boy. Big sister, Brenda, who was in one of the higher grades at the same elementary school "got wind" of the abuse to her younger brother and "took care of" and "administrated some justice" to that bully. Keith no longer had any bully problems, swing problems, or any other such problems at school because of his older sister's, Brenda's, care and justice. All in all, to this day, if Brenda decides to "step up to any plate," all say she will succeed in hitting a homerun.

"Sewer Rat"

Speaking of Keith...Keith brings up the rear of Dorothy's children. He is the youngest, only in his early forties, being born April 26, 1967 in DePaul Hospital, here in Cheyenne, when his mother was already forty-four years old. There are twelve years between James Jr. and Keith, eleven years between Kathy and Keith, and even three years between Brenda and Keith. Not only was the age of

Dorothy when Keith was born unique, but also the circumstances around his "birthing." Keith would be James Sr. and Dorothy's fourth, and final, child. However, if Dorothy had given birth to all of the children she had conceived she would have actually given birth to eight children. Dorothy had another two miscarriages around the time of Keith's birth, one just before and even a last one, after.

Many unique circumstances surrounded Keith's birth including a cousin, Leola's daughter, Tina, being born just a month later than Keith. One of the more entertaining elements of Keith's birth was his doctor, little Dr. Pelley. Dr. Pelley, especially since he was from Texas, should have put more stock in "old Southern tales," particularly related to his field of childbirth. It is possible if he had believed Dorothy and her Southern lore about "babies being born according to the moon," he may have come to the hospital in time to deliver Keith. Instead, Dorothy would basically deliver Keith independent of medical help. Dr. Pelley would later compare Dorothy to a Philippine woman the doctor had seen literally "go into a rice field, drop the baby, cut her own cord with her teeth, shed her own afterbirth, and then continue walking down the path with her baby now in her arms." Later, Dr. Pelley would teasingly apologize to Dorothy about her solo delivery by telling her to "go ahead and take the baby down to the nursery yourself, too. You do not need to be scared. You did everything else by yourself." Dorothy did as the doctor ordered, even though she was terrified enough that her "knees were popping." Dorothy was especially concerned about the reaction of the two older ladies, come to visit someone else, as they watched her shakily carry her infant down the hall. She knew what she had to do, though. She must carry her own baby because she was not sure if the Sisters (Nuns) at this Catholic hospital could hold babies for the patients, or not, since they could not have their own babies. She was never told the answer to that, but she did later learn that they (the Sisters) are bald, with heads shaved under their wimples.

In spite of Dorothy's fear of dropping Keith at the hospital, she need not have worried about a baby spill at the hospital. It did not happen there. However, Keith jokes about being dropped on his head as a baby. He even adds that family member's tease about his being dropped on the hard oak floor at home and that is why his head is so hard. However, he does not necessarily blame his mother for the "dropping." He thinks it was probably one of the older children. Another injury Keith experienced when he was small was a furnace burn. This one was not to his head, but more in the groin area. Dorothy also was not the cause of this, but more of a witness. Keith was learning to go potty, had not fully redressed, came running for help, tripped on the open furnace appliances being cleaned, and hurt himself. He was burned, but not enough to cause permanent damage. However, no matter how "earth-shattering" these early events in Keith's life may have been, Keith, himself, probably due to his age when these events occurred, told of other childhood events as more, or the most, memorable to him.

These most memorial events for Keith, as a child, were actually of getting in trouble. His was described as the "generation of the switch from the tree," probably most likely because his parents were still from an older generation. His mother believed in that "old school" discipline being already forty-four years old before Keith was even born. Dorothy, herself, adds, when questioned about her strictness, "Yes, I was a more-mature mother and a Southern, Black one at that." Specifically, Keith admits to receiving a "behind switching" many times and even having to make his own switches to be used. In his own words, he added "most were made for Mom but the biggest ones were for Dad." Additionally, Keith agrees with the saying "that a sore behind holds the most vivid memories."

It was because of his Sunday schooling experiences that actually lead to one of Keith's more-memorable "butt-chewing's," though. During several weeks of his elementary Sunday School days, Keith decided to visit the City News bookstore to read the Superman comics and skip out of Sunday School. (The First AME Allen Chapel was just across the street from the bookstore at the time.) Needless-to-say, as soon as Mom, and later Dad, found out about the missed Sunday School from the deserted Sunday School teacher, the behavior almost instantly stopped. From that day on, Superman never beat out Jonah and the Whale again. Although Keith then reiterated that he is sure to this day that his own youthful bottom felt less punished than Jonah's adult body felt after being swallowed by a whale.

However, to this day, Keith does not regret the strict discipline from his childhood. Contrarily, he attributes his "old-fashioned upbringing" to his later success as an adult. Keith even said that "being held back in 3rd grade was the best thing to happen" to him because "that year was when he actually learned to read." Fortunately, for Keith with this "tough love," Keith not only learned to do well in school, Sunday School, and finally, when to work and when to play. Keith was especially good at playing basketball. He replaced his fictional idol of Superman with the real idols of Magic Johnson and Michael Jordan. For high school and junior college, Keith became locally known for the "thrown ball in the basket."

Truthfully, like most little brothers, the best "playing" for Keith was "playing with the big boys." Keith just thought that doing anything athletic, football and basketball, or just "hanging with the boys" was a childhood highlight of any younger brother, particularly one twelve years younger than his older brother. He also loved to hunt rabbits, birds, and big game with the guys, even when Keith could not keep his first killed antelope because the family only had two licenses, not three. Keith emphasized how the brothers were above all "big shots with ducks." Especially since there was just not as much technology back then, Keith additionally remembers all of "the guys watching less TV and more riding bikes" everywhere from the 7-11 to Gibson's and even to Grand Central. (None of which even still exist in any form now.)

When specifically asked what Keith remembers most about growing up with Dorothy as a mother, Keith just like his brother, James Jr., also remembers family. First, he remembered how his Aunt Leola still had her Southern Black accent while his mother only used a few "pet Southern left-over" terms such as calling all his friends and acquaintances "darlings." Although the boys were often called "Darling" or "Pet" from Keith's 70 year old

Southern Black mother, they were not offended, but actually endeared more to Keith. Plus, they all knew that Keith's mom refused to lag behind any of their "younger moms." Dorothy always was, even to Keith's peers, and still is, "get up and get it done Dorothy."

The special family traditions that Keith remembered most also were of family. One was of the Christmas that big-brother, James, after he was up late cruising, that "Mom got James up early so he could set up the car racing track for his younger-brother, me." That same day, they even had races on that train set. Keith did not know for years that it was "rigged" when he, the new train owner, actually beat big brother in every race with the new set.

It was from work that Keith earned the nickname of "Sewer Rat." Because of his job with the water department and even now, Keith is teasingly compared to Norton, the Sewer Rat, from the Honeymooners. The nickname came when he started with the Cheyenne Water Department during the summers of 1984 and 85, and for the years afterward, he worked on the "sewer side" of the department. Keith was officially hired as a "sewer rat" in 1988 through a JTPA, minority hiring initiative. For him, this was a definite step up from sweeping curbs at Little America. Fifteen years later, Keith is still called "Sewer Rat," but his title of more respect should be "Maintenance Rat "now. In 1993 he tested for the "manual on machines" and after passing he transferred to maintenance on the water side. In his years with the water department, Keith has not only been a hard worker but a positive reflection of his Hayes family upbringing, his own moral character, and very much a good example of Black dignity and goodness. Plus, he gets the privilege of being outdoors all of the time with the trees and nature he knows and loves.

When asked about race issues, Keith responded just as expected--being someone that had Dorothy as a mother. Keith spoke of an environment growing up where all of the family just "tried to mix and mingle" with everyone else. He especially remembers parents who were "not too ignorant" and taught their children not to be hateful and look past color. Unfortunately, that did not prevent Keith from being discriminated against, especially since he was the "trophy Black employee" at the water plant for many years. Once after moving to the "water side" of the department, he heard a fellow worker speak of his "nigger pay." He mostly ignored the jibe and the person from that day forward. However, this comment did take him back to a high school basketball game in Gillette, Wyoming, where the opponents were freely speaking of the "Jungle Bunny" and "Mr. Taco" players visiting from Cheyenne.

High school was not usually a bad memory for Keith. In fact, it was at Central High School where he met his High School Sweetheart, Senovia. Senovia was born in Las Vegas in 1968 (They met in 1986 as sophomores because Keith was held back and Senovia moved in.) They dated through high school, and endured a long distance romance after while they both went to different colleges, until they married September 21, 1989. They were married by the Justice of the Peace and had a quiet reception at the NCO (Non-commissioned Officers) club. Their first of two daughters was Desiree (Desi) born during March of 1990 and during a common spring blizzard. Finally, after twenty-one hours of labor, Dr Eskam, took the 8 lb, 21 oz Desi by C-section. Only after becoming a parent first hand did Keith completely understand how much Dorothy "had it figured out as a Mom." Today, he only wants to thank her for being the mother she was.

"Grandma Dora"

All of Dorothy's children, including Keith, specifically mentioned vivid memories of their Grandma Dora, (Idora James), Dorothy's very strong-willed mother. Seeing Grandma Dora was most often the object of their youthful travels. Dorothy, James Sr. and the children traveled a lot "when work allowed" as a young family, particularly to see Idora, and other members of the extended family, many of whom were still in the South. Because Grandma Dora was such a lively personality to see, Keith, colorfully spoke of first going to seeing Grandma Dora in an old rented Winnebago with Willie James, (Dorothy's brother), and the Denver cousins. Keith even admits that it was startling to meet his grandmother this first time. She did not expect their visit and met the intruders with a gun and bearded stance that the then-youthful Keith even now distinctly visualizes.

Additionally, and fortunately for James Jr., on another visit to Grandma Dora's, James did not realize at the time how drastic his city naiveté could have proven. It was not until after his Grandma Dora stepped in that it all became clear. In his own words, James described the incident like this: "When we went to my grandparent's farm I thought this Jackass was a horse. My grandma came to the rescue. I was behind the horse not knowing he was getting ready to kill me. I was petting him and he raised his tail leg to strike me." It had been only because of Grandma Dora's fast removal of James from the position he was in that truthfully saved him from a deadly kick.

In truth, Hayes family vacations most often were taken to the "great outdoors" or to visit family members, including Grandma Dora. Daughter Kathy remembers family vacations in this way: "We're not the Disney kind of family. We like the great outdoors: camping, fishing, and hunting. One summer weekend, my brothers and sister and I wanted to pack for our camping weekend. We were so happy and proud of ourselves until dinner time. We forgot the skillet, the spatula, and a big, big fork. So mom, being mom, said, 'Oh well, let's go buy them.' To this day she still has that skillet. Also, I remember another vacation when we went on the train to Louisiana or Mississippi and I got sick. I felt so bad. Mom felt bad. All the passengers felt bad."

Finally, even granddaughter, Pernisha, described vacationing with the Hayes family like this: "My grandpa worked for the U.P. and received train tickets all the time. So almost every summer my grandma would take us somewhere. I loved those trips because we traveled by train and the scenery was beautiful. I learned a lot about life on those trips because life everyplace else but Wyoming was exciting and different. My grandparents made sure we were exposed to how life really is and the different kinds and types of people there are in the world. I'm fortunate that we have family all around the U.S. and we have visited most. My grandparents made sure we knew our family."

Then Pernisha added, "when I was little (actually even before I was born) my grandparents would go on fishing trips to various lakes around Wyoming and

Nebraska. Our immediate family would meet up with our extended family (my grandparents, cousins, nieces and nephews) from Colorado with their RV's and we'd make a weekend! We would fish, cook, play, party, eat, and dance to the music! Notice I didn't mention sleep—didn't do much of that!"

After Dorothy's father, Joseph James, died and Idora, her mother, needed more care, travel to see Grandma Dora became much simpler for the Hayes family. Idora came to Cheyenne, Wyoming to live and be cared for by her two daughters living there, Dorothy and Leola. In fact, Idora lived in Cheyenne until 1983 when she passed away. Idora kept her Southern Black spunk until the day she died complete with blisters on her fingers from smoking and, even up until the day that she died, calling deserving people at the hospital and care center "Son of a b..."

Speaking of the day Idora died, Dorothy tells of the following scenario. As Dorothy left her mother's side at

Cheyenne's Eventide Nursing Home to go to work that particular November day in 1983, she could just sense something odd. In fact, as she left her mother's sleeping bedside to say good-bye until after work, the doctor interrupted her. He just simply stated that "your mother will die today between 5:00 and 5:30 p.m., so plan accordingly." Ironically, that very day, as if fulfilling a prophecy, Idora James did pass away at 5:15 p.m. just as the doctor had predicted. Also, as if ending an era, Dorothy, who usually took care of her mother in the evenings, was there to send this once strong, but always God-fearing, woman to meet her Maker. However, all who knew Idora James, or now know her descendants, see the remnant of her faith still coursing through all of their souls. Many of which are of varying denominations, but all share some sort of belief. This is Idora's legacy that "all have some belief, but that belief can be 'to each his own' with respect for any other and their own belief."

"Faith: Land versus Water"

Dorothy is a walking epiphany of her mother's "legacy of faith." She literally wears a T-shirt that reads "We walk by faith not by sight" (II Corinthians 5:7)—an outward witness of her faith. Additionally, not many birthdays past, because her birthday fell on the Sabbath, Dorothy's only birthday present wish was to have all of her kids (children and grandchildren included) at church with her. For those living in Cheyenne that wish was able to be fulfilled.

Granddaughter Ashley Rambo from Washington State tells of coming to visit Cheyenne and also sharing Dorothy's church-going Sunday ritual with her grandmother: "When Sunday morning arrives, Grandma drags us out of bed for church. 'Comb out that nappy head, come now, gets da stepping,' she insists. Church is located just a couple blocks away from the house. The kids stumble in through the doors in a tired, sleepy haze.

Gospel music fills the room, as the small gathering of Black faces sing with soul and pride. After we've been seated, the pastor starts shouting, 'Can I get an Amen!' Once when a lady had fainted, some people started fanning her off with the supplied fans. 'This woman is feeling the power of the Lord,' stated the pastor. Voices shout from every direction 'Hal Aula!' (Hallelujah), 'Amen!', and "Praise the Lord!' At closing prayer time, I silently make sure to add a blessing for the wonderful family I was given."

It is important to note that Dorothy was not a lone Christian and that James Sr. found, and also accepted, Jesus on Easter in 1955, never leaving Dorothy to worship alone from that day forward. It is told that Easter is always one of the most special and holy days for all Christians. In 1955, Easter was not to be only a traditionally religious day but also to be a most thrilling day for the Hayes family as well. James Jr. was to be, and was, christened. James Sr.

also surprised the family by requesting to be, and was baptized, that day as well. James Sr. had attended church some, and been a believer before but the complete commitment to Allen Chapel, and the African Methodist faith, was a wonderful blessing, and "positively life-changing" for all involved.

The couple, and the family, remained righteous from that date on, and most still attend the same Allen Chapel of Cheyenne (the African- American Methodist Episcopal congregation) of James Sr.'s conversion. It is particular note that the same year this book was written was when Allen Chapel of Cheyenne celebrated its 130th anniversary, making for a wonderful historical coincidence. In fact, Pernisha Hayes, (the granddaughter that "wore the crown perfectly" when she did the "Wedding of Roses" as a child), was then, and still is, a very faithful and active member in Allen Chapel, even being pictured in the Cheyenne Wyoming Tribune Eagle with the following article about this aforementioned and eventful anniversary celebration: "Church visitors and congregation members sing and clap during the church's celebration. The church was established in1867 when Wyoming was still a territory. It was the first African American church in the state and continues its ministry 130 years later. The church, as a connectional member of the African Methodist Episcopal Church, is part of the oldest organization of any kind established by African Americans in the United States. Sunday's celebration included pastors from neighboring churches as well as guest choirs." *--Brandon Quester/staff*

Many things have changed in the 130 years of Allen Chapel including their recently-ordained woman pastor although the tenants remain enough the same for Dorothy "to feel right at home even after these many years." In fact, Dorothy is a woman of power in the congregation, being a "stewardess." A statement from the stewardess women themselves described them as "very privileged, blessed, and humble to serve as your stewardesses. Ordinary women engaged in extraordinary work in God's Love." As a stewardess, Dorothy is pictured at the church. Some of Dorothy's fellow attendees have been known to look at her picture and say that her photo looks almost "saint-like." Also, many church members, or even neighbors and acquaintances, bring their Christian debates to Dorothy's advice table because whether Dorothy is truly a saint in literal terms may be debated but functional terms it is not considered debatable. In particular, Pernisha defined her grandmother's morals, and what she learned personally from growing up in her grandmother's home, this way: "My family has taught me to admire people who are about something. Morals, ethics, and Southern tradition are high on our list. People who work hard, stand up for what is right, would rather give than receive, look out for one another, and don't beat around the bush are highly respected and admired in my household. With that in mind, we should all surround ourselves around people with such qualities and characteristics. Plus, if they weren't, or my family could sense that they ain't right, they were told or got the hint and never were invited, nor invite themselves back to our house. It turned out that ten times out of ten assumptions were right!"

Dorothy may have chosen to become Methodist like her family growing up, but was not practicing that religion for the first few years in Cheyenne mostly because she had not yet found a Methodist congregation to worship with. She even attended the Second Baptist Church of Cheyenne with her first local landlord, and even today "fesses up" that the Baptists do have better music although Methodist's prayers are just as good. (Dorothy added "This is very important when your family is as large as mine and you need to pray for so many.") Additionally, her sister, Leola still is an actively practicing member of The Second Baptist Church of Cheyenne. "Land vs. water" can still be a phrase of slight contention with these two sisters. "Land is for the Methodists who sprinkle, and Water is for the Baptists who immerse."

However, these sisters contend less about hats than about religion. Black women of both of their faiths definitely wear hats with the same fervor. Interestingly, Dorothy could do nothing but agree with the following quote taken from the book <u>Crowns, Portraits of Black Women in Church Hats:</u> "More than a simple fashion statement, the hats worn by Black women to church were a declaration of having arrived…A lot of people have always considered the hats as being a mere fashion statement, but it started out as a symbol of independence and freedom. Women would work for six days a week and then lay out their Sunday clothes on Saturday night. But they would wait until Sunday morning to select the hat they were going to wear. That late choice…was to make sure the hat matched the attitude…Some women became so attached to their hats they even insisted on being buried in them…"

Specifically, the article adds the following about the traditions of Black women and hats: "The tradition of women wearing hats goes back to an interpretation of the Bible passage in 1 Corinthians 11:5: 'And every woman who prays or prophesies with her head uncovered dishonors her head, it is just as though her head were shaved.'… That is what led to the tradition…In addition to the scripture verse…the tradition dated back to the days of slavery…Those ladies only had a bandanna to wear around their heads…so they would dress them up with flowers and other special touches to make them personal and unique. The hats we wear now are in part a continuation of that tradition…And you can be sure each has at least one hat…Every color and every style will be on display. But you have to remember that the hats are not for self-glorification but for the glorification of God" (Halvorson).

Just as this article indicates, both James sisters, Dorothy and Leola, frequently wear hats to church. At the present, Leola often wears hats of a little fancier brand than Dorothy, just because of age. Back when Dorothy first moved to Cheyenne she did have her first fancy "store-bought" Sunday get-up. She still remembers the matching red hat, gloves, and shoes brought from, and bought in, California. Now, she likes little box hats that just sit atop her head because her face is too small for the big showcase ones. Plus, these hats can be purchased at Good Will for much more reasonable prices.

"I'm just Nobody Trying to help Somebody"

Dorothy may "cut corners" with expenditures when related to the culture of church, but when making purchases with the welfares of the soul, no expense is too much. With Dorothy's life, all are sure she sees eye-to-eye with the Delany sisters when they say: "I'll tell you a little secret: I'm starting to get optimistic. I'm thinking; maybe I'll get into Heaven after all. Why, I've helped a lot of folks—even some white folks! I surely do have some redeeming qualities that must count for something. So I just might do it; I just might get into Heaven. I may have to hang on to someone's heels, but I'll get there" (299).

When it comes to living a Christian life, especially when dealing with family members, Dorothy truly would, and does, give her all just like the following song suggests. The song is called "I'm Just a Nobody Trying to help Somebody" and quite possibly could be called Dorothy's theme song. It was recorded in the 1980s by The Williams Brothers and goes like this:

Intro:
I was walking downtown one day, and I saw a man that appeared to be just an old wino; sitting on the streets, telling the people about Jesus as they passed by.
And because he was all raggedy and dirty, people would just laugh and make fun of the old man and walk on by.
And he said that because of the way I am, no money, no fancy clothes, no fine homes and cars, a lot of people consider me a nothing, and say I don't know what I am talking about.

But there is one thing that he said that really touched my heart and stayed on my mind, when that old man looked up and said...
Chorus:
I'm just a nobody trying to tell everybody, about somebody, who can save anybody.
I'm just a nobody trying to tell everybody, about somebody, who can save anybody
Verse 1:
And he added, "I've had so many problems in my life that I just couldn't deal with so I started drinking, thought it would help ease my pain.
But things got worse, so I said, 'Lord I give up. I'm in your hands', and that's when my life began to change, but these people think..."
Chorus:
Verse 2:
Then he said, "On the streets day and night, that's my life, that's my home, ain't got nowhere else I could go.
So I just walk the streets, telling the people about Jesus from corner to corner, from door to door;
But they all make fun of me and say..."
Chorus:

The first, and most obvious, way that Dorothy shows daily that she truly does as this song preaches of "saving anyone" is in the daily "love and saving" she offers to each of her grandchildren. Dorothy knows that it is to her benefit to give back to family, particularly the children. She simply says, "When you're nice to kids, they're nice to you." Because of this special grandmother and grandchild bond, it was not difficult to get many special words from, and about, Dorothy's grandchildren. Also, even though Dorothy's oldest granddaughter, Monika, left her father James Jr. when she was eight, and is now thirty-six, Dorothy's philosophy with her and all of her grandchildren was, and is, "my door is always open."

This theory has come into practice many times, as has been seen with all of Dorothy's progenitors, except the above-mentioned Monika. However, Dorothy continues to pray that someday that will even occur, especially because, until very recently, this Monika was "the first grandchild and was also the only grandchild to produce the great-grandkids." When specifically asked about this granddaughter, Kathy added the following: "Wow! Mom has a lot of grand babies and now great-grand babies, too. Monika, the first born, my brother, James' child, I met her once. She was ten or eleven and looked like him."

Kathy went on by saying "Pernisha, the second grandchild, having her in my life is great. She made me an aunt and I liked that. She also made me to want to be a mother. She is outspoken, smart, funny, talented, making me a great aunt. People in the family say that Pernisha should be my child. We do look alike." Pernisha is Brenda's daughter, but because of the circumstances surrounding her birth, she also lived with her grandparents all of growing up years. Pernisha's father was a married man from on the base who did not ever leave his wife and marry Pernisha's mother. Even though her father never lived with her, he was always very good to Pernisha and did have some contact with her. However, it ended up being Dorothy and James Sr. that did many parental tasks for, and with, Pernisha, including buying her first dress and helping raise her at 2719 Bent Ave.

Pernisha specifically remembers the winter holidays of Thanksgiving, Dr. Martin Luther King Jr. Day, and

Easter as a member of the Hayes household. Additionally, she detailed Christmas this way: "Christmas as a child was great! The house was decked out in Christmas decorations. The house had this certain Christmas aroma that was only smelled at Christmas time! I can't deeply put my finger on it, but you know it was definitely that time of year." Then, Saturdays and vacation days "were normal kick-back days, where cleaning was done and sleep might get caught up on."

About Pernisha's grandparents and her childhood friend, Pernisha told: "My childhood friend/best friend (adopted by love and spirit) was, and still is, Suaese (Val) Sevi. (For pronunciation purposes we'll call him Val) Val and I met in fourth grade. He made a lasting first impression. We would get out of school (elementary) at 3:15 p.m., and he would walk home with me and my grandpa, who picked me up every day. Then, we would drop him off, too. Val stayed around the corner from our school. By the time I got home, he would have already called! After I was home, he would keep calling like we were old folks who hadn't talked in years, every time! My grandma would say: 'Why does he call so much?' Irritated, my grandpa was worse; he'd ask Val why he called so much, every time he called, and say 'oh boy' and a few 'got damns.' Let's say, Val used to be terrified of my grandpa! As years went by, our friendship became stronger and our families were known to each other. When we were in high school, our families were very persistent on us dating. We were too close to ever be a couple, though. From junior high on, we had called ourselves brother and sister. My grandpa and grandma grew to love him as their grandson and respected and valued our relationship. My grandparents would always say 'He's a good kid. I like Val.' Mom always called him, 'my other son!' His parents referred to me as his wife: 'Val, your wife called' or 'your wife is home.' And it was funny every time!"

All of the family, including Pernisha, showed great attachments to the family pets. Kathy told the following about the Hayes pets: "As long as I can remember we had had pets. Rabbits, chickens, turtles, birds, cats, and of course, dogs. The one that sticks out the most was Sam, the green parrot, my eldest brother's pet. Sam thought he was human. He would exercise with Brenda. He also was bald-breasted from tapping on the door to get in after he snuck out. Another pet of James Isaac Hayes (he always had the most interesting of the pets) was a little, black and, wiry dog that was so cute. He would sit on your face if you didn't wake up to let him out. Sparkie, (Rex to some), the face-sitter, got hit by a train at Buford. He would sit on the train tracks. Therefore, we were always worried that he would, in the end, encounter the end that he did. Mom loved that dog. My dog, after I was grown, was a girl German Shepherd, Brownie, my so-called 'watch dog.' I would hear something outside, let Brownie out and she would run, not walk, to my mother's house and stay there.

"However, I think everyone's favorite pet, if not only mine, was Bumper, half and half of something. He was small dog, but with a Big Dog Attitude. He would sleep on Mom and Dad's bed, on furniture, or wherever he wanted. He would climb the tree in the backyard and then couldn't get down. Sometimes, he would come home all beat up. He had a record at the Humane Society for fighting. The Humane Society would even call the house letting us know they had him. Mom would tell them, 'You can keep him.' She'd then add, 'I am so tired of bailing this dog out.' Nonetheless, by the end of that day, Bumper would be home."

It was Pernisha that told the following "Bumper pet scenario," though: "When I was a little girl, (I was seven years old), our family dog Bumper died. After school that day was when I found out. I changed into my church clothes and Uncle Keith, my grandpa, my mom and my grandma had a funeral for him in the alley. I sang a song and said a prayer. My uncle officiated at the funeral. It was a sad day, but my antics definitely made the family laugh. Thinking about it now, reminds our family of The Cosby Show episode when Rudy had a funeral for her goldfish" (Goodbye Mr. Fish).

It is very enlightening that Pernisha has such a positive outlook on her life growing up because she actually was "the miracle baby that tested the faith of the family at an early age." At the age of three she was diagnosed with cancer and had a kidney removed at the Shriner's Hospital in Salt Lake City, Utah. Dorothy commented that she would have liked any of her own surgeries done at the Shriner's Hospital, as well. They were just "the kindest people ever" and the facilities were "so clean you could eat off the floor."

Pernisha described her own illness in these words: "What's special about me is that I'm the second grandchild born to the family and the sickly one--always ill as a child, grandchild. When I was three years old, I was diagnosed with Wilms tumor (cancer) and was then deathly sick. Later on in life, I was told I wasn't supposed to live past five years old. Here I am at twenty-seven years and writing about my grandma. Being sick had its advantages though. I was spoiled by everyone! I thought I've grown out of it, but people: my mom, uncles, aunts, and cousins, say that I'm still the same spoiled brat. I disagree!"

After Pernisha, came granddaughter Ashley Hayes who is the only granddaughter in the Rambo family and also "the first grandkid to graduate college." Currently, she is in New York City studying music. Her mother, Kathy, described her as "my Ashley, the third grandchild and my little girl. Ashley is a joy! Her sense of adventure, no fear, she gets that from Grandma. I hadn't seen my mom since

Senovia died in 2005, so when Ashley graduated from PSU (Pacific State University) in 2008 she flew Mom here for five wonderful days. I was so happy and proud of her. She has always been a writer, too." This is one of the first writings that Ashley created as a young child and sent to Dorothy for Mother's (Grandmother's) Day:

Grandmother--

Your love so sweet

Your strength so strong

In my heart is where you'll always belong

A mother (a grandmother) looked up to

By all that love

You bring us—I'm thankful for.

Have a wonderful day!

—Ashley Collin Hayes Rambo

The next grandchild (fourth grandchild) is Matthew Rambo. Matthew is a Mormon convert and was a missionary. Dorothy, while he was serving his mission, described him this way: "Matthew is a missionary in North Carolina and a true man of God." She was only teasingly worried that he would come home with a Southern accent, although she was so pleased that he "loves it so much and is so happy, maybe I should be a Mormon, too," she still jokes. His mother, Kathy, also while he was gone, agreed with Dorothy by saying: "Matthew is Mom and Dad's first-born grandson. Mattie, his nickname, is a good son, good person, loving, and talented. He is the artist. He is serving an LDS mission in North Carolina. He will be home in April." (Matthew did honorably complete his mission in April 2009 while this book was being written.)

Kathy went on to talk about Desi, Keith's daughter, the number five grandchild, and then Eli. Desi "is my little brother's first child. She started bringing so much joy even when she was born. She is gifted like both her parents and is a jewel. My baby is Eli, the number six grandchild. He and Desi are one month apart. Desi was born in March, Eli in April. My baby, I wanted to hold on to him as long as I could. He is so sweet, very straight forward, speaks his mind, and is a very gifted young man." Currently, Desi is working "partly, to help her dad" and heading toward the military or the fire department after graduating from high school last spring. Desi will do well with whatever she does because Grandma Dorothy knows that she "demonstrates strength and courage from all she has been, and will go, through." Eli will also make it through these tough post-high school years, especially since he has that red-head disposition. Dorothy said, "I, grandma, nicknamed him carrot head because his hair is red and still is to this day."

Kathy continues with "Isaiah, grandchild number seven, is my sister's only son. I love him so much. I remember, when Brenda was pregnant with him, she was so big. She thought he was coming the first part of

September. I told her 'no way, girl.' I know he is coming nearer the end of September. She got mad. He came late and I won. He is a 'Big Boy with Big Heart.' I look forward to seeing him in the summer—He is going to be something BIG, wait and see." Because Isaiah is "so big," both physically and spiritually, Grandmother Dorothy even calls Isaiah, Rock head. This nickname first came because of his huge, bald baby head. Today, this nickname seems even more appropriate since he is a twelve-year-old, seventh grader at McCormick playing football and especially because of his size 15 shoes that are special ordered for $176 in Loveland, Colorado. Dorothy adds, "Isaiah expresses great enthusiasm for family and mankind. He has a big heart and loves life. He wants to make a difference in the world." This became particularly obvious when Isaiah articulated in school that he wanted to be, partly for his grandpa, President of United States. The teacher expressed more concern, however, when Isaiah then changed his mind because he believed he could not do so, being the wrong color. The teacher's reply came as "Isaiah, you tell your grandpa that you want to be President, and that I say you can be anything you want." Dorothy said this incident was an "essential lesson" that had to be told of, and for, her grandson, or any other Black child. "It must be included in the book," she concluded, emphatically.

Finally, Kathy ends with "and of course, there is our little Tianna. She is sweet and cute. When I was here in 2005, we, her and I, had a tea party. It was called 'Tea with Tianna at Ten.' She loved that so much. We had another tea party later with other family members and friends. She is going to be a little Miss Social-life. All of my mother and father's grand children are a continuation of them both. We are so blessed!"

Tianna is a "dainty little lady, who takes care of, and carries, herself as a lady." She is known for wearing a tiara at the cousin's wedding, always dancing and singing, plus being the "girl of girls." She frequently questions her dad with sayings such as: "Dad, can I wear this boot and skirt?" Then, to her grandmother make the statement "I can style!" In Dorothy's own words, "Tianna definitely keeps the ball rollin'." This is Tianna's own story of what she remembers most about having Grandma Dorothy: "When I went to my family reunion, that's when I and my grandma had a good time together. We did not have much food. There were a lot of people. That's how come we did not have a lot of food to eat. My grandma said, 'See, I can't do this.' I said, 'We have to.' Then, my grandma said 'No, not me. I have to eat.' So, that night, before they saw us, she and I got a sandwich and went back to sleep. The next day, my grandma offered to do the food, but they said that they now had gotten more food. So, I went to play and my grandma went to see the family. Also, we danced and sang.

So that's when grandma and I had a good time. I loved that time so much!"

"Just too Young"

Another situation for which Dorothy has sacrificed more than just "material possessions, time, and the freedom of 'old age," and also includes "saving someone," directly relates back to the aforementioned of Dorothy's grandchildren. Specially, it pertains to her son, Keith, the death of his young wife, Senovia, and their daughters, and her granddaughters, Desiree and Tianna, who were still of minor age at the time of their mother's death. Senovia, Dorothy's young (30-something) daughter-in-law dead prematurely after years of illness in 2005. Dorothy vowed at her daughter-in-law's (Senovia's) death that she would do, and still does, whatever she can for her son and granddaughters which were left behind. Even today, Dorothy reminds people she has to continue on as said in her own words "I'll need to be around ...'cause I need to help raise Keith's kids."

Ironically, Dorothy had a sister-in-law that also "passed on" at a very young age, in her thirties. This woman, however, died in a car crash driving home to California from Las Vegas while her husband, Dorothy's brother was only scratched. Even in her later years, Dorothy has not come to understand why some are taken so young, and others, like her, are "allowed to continue through so much for so much longer." Although with the time, she has been granted, she has tried to fill the gap left by those taken. This she has done so well since the beginning, when she presented one of her "famous church readings" at her daughter-in-law's funeral, and it continues on to this day. The following is that previously-mentioned reading and another affirmation of Dorothy's unwavering faith:

"Heaven's Grocery Store"
"I was walking down life's highway a long time age. One day I saw a sign that read Heaven's Grocery store. As I got a little close, the door came open wide, and when I came to myself, I was standing inside.
I saw a host of angels, they were standing everywhere. One handed me a basket and said 'my child, shop with care.'
Everything a Christian needed was in that Grocery Store, and all you couldn't carry, you could come back the next day for more.
First, I got some Patience; Love was in the same row. Further down was Understanding. You need that everywhere you go.
I got a box or two of Wisdom, a box or two of Faith; I just couldn't miss the Holy Ghost, for it was all over the place.
I stopped to get some Strength and Courage to help me run this race. By then my basket was getting full, but I remembered I needed some Grace.
I didn't forget Salvation, for Salvation that was free...So I tried to get enough of that to save both you and me. Then I started up to the counter, to pay my grocery bill. For I thought I had everything to do my Master's will.
As I went up the aisle, I saw Prayer and I just had to put that in...For I knew when I stepped outside, I would run right into sin. Peace and Joy were plentiful; they were on the last shelf. Songs and Praises were handing near, so I just helped myself.
Then I said to the angel: 'Now, how much do I owe?' He just smiled and said, 'just take them everywhere you go.' Again I smiled at him and said, 'How much, now, do I really owe?"
He smiled again and said, 'My child Jesus paid your bill a long time ago.'"

Additionally, Dorothy was, and is, so grateful that good Christian people, Black and White, on this side of the veil, have been there to console her, and hers, in days of distress, particularly surrounding Senovia's "early death." In actuality, Keith was warned to pay close attention to how many people, many White, were there to hug, and do for him, at Senovia's funeral and the days following. In fact, Dorothy teased Keith that day that he has not before, and probably will not ever again "be hugged by so many White people." (Probably before that day, he did not realize how many White people he even knew, let alone that he could hug.) We, the Dobsons, were some of those. It was because of Senovia working for my husband and his doctor's office that we came to know and love Senovia, Keith, and particularly Dorothy. Yes, Dorothy worked for, and still does work for, us by cleaning our house. She has also cleaned for a lot of other people in Cheyenne, some of them prominent members of the community. More on us, and the many families, blessed by having Dorothy working in their homes, is coming later.

"Keep on Workin'"

Because Dorothy was born a sharecropper's daughter, and started working in the plantation fields almost from the time she could walk, she has spent all but a very few years of her existence in the work force. Additionally, Dorothy, like most of Black America, was part of the manual labor force. As pointed out in this quote, though, Dorothy "did a good show" for herself as an employee. "The rebby boys don't give colored folks credit for a thing, not a single thing. Why I think we've done pretty well, considering we were dragged over here in chains from Africa! Why colored folks built this country and that is the truth. We were the laborers, honey! And even after we were freed, we were the backbone of this country—the maids, cooks, undertakers, barbers, porters, and so on" (Delany 16). Unlike some Blacks who have only complained about it, Dorothy is "used to working for the 'white folks'" and is not negative about them, overall.

In her opinion, her White employers "all have been good to her." Probably, partly because of this, even into her eighties, Dorothy plans to work as long as she can. She claims that she actually "loves to work" because she has "no patience for just sitting around…always gotta move, and go to work."

During her years of employment, Dorothy has spent most of them as a cleaning lady. Because of this, the following excerpt from the prose piece, <u>Five Important Lessons,</u> seems so applicable to her:

"The Cleaning Lady"

"During my second month of college, our professor gave us a pop quiz. I was a conscientious student and had breezed through the questions until I read the last one:
'What is the first name of the woman who cleans the school?'
Surely this was some kind of joke. I had seen the cleaning woman several times. She was tall, dark-haired and in her 50's, but how would I know her name?
I handed in my paper, leaving the last question blank. Just before class ended, one student asked if the last question would count toward our quiz grade.

'Absolutely,' said the professor, 'in your careers, you will meet many people. All are significant. They deserve your attention and care, even if all you do is smile and say 'hello.'
I've never forgotten that lesson. I also learned her name was Dorothy."

During her years of cleaning in Cheyenne, Dorothy has been employed by many prominent and influential families. Her first job was with the Waldmans. They were Kosher Jews with a ball-shaped house downtown on Central Avenue. This family she specifically remembered using a set of silver for every meal. Therefore, the silver needed polished each week. Additionally, the family owned a men's store where Dorothy was required weekly to dust all of the shoes sitting on the shelves.

Her second employer, but not necessarily in time or priority, was the Johnsons. They have since moved and "gone." The father was a pilot. The son which Dorothy once babysat, grew up to be a lawyer, and is now a judge. In fact, Mrs. Johnson and Dorothy, herself, were pregnant at same time. The lady of the house claimed their pregnancies must be due to "the water" since this was her third child and a long awaited first child for Dorothy.

A third employer was the Smiths. Dorothy still cleans for this mother of twins, but the twins, Amy and Anne, have since moved to California to sing professionally. Of these Smith twins, who were still very young at the time, Dorothy tells of their self-started house fire. Dorothy also recalls having to both help save the house from permanent destruction and later punish the girls for their immature behavior.

Fourth was the Troutwines. He was president of the bank that was then across from a Chinese restaurant. (President Troutwine is not to be confused with President Walters of a competing bank for whom Dorothy also worked. Mr. Walters has since passed away even though he was the same age as Dorothy. His wife has married since and only summers here in a townhouse and winters in

Texas.) To Dorothy, the Troutwines are best known for their eight bathrooms. Because of the size of the house, Dorothy went twice a week to clean there. It was the upstairs on Wednesday and downstairs on Friday. The Troutwines were the "Country Club" types always playing bridge, having fancy birthday parties into the night, and the like. Ironically, Mrs. Troutwine was Jewish and Mr. Troutwine was German. To this day, Dorothy is not sure why this family, although not small, actually needed eight bathrooms since all four of their children were "B- named" boys.

Speaking of presidents, Dorothy not only worked for two bank presidents, but also for the president of Taco Johns Corporation and the associate president of Taco Johns. This assistant president's wife was so Southern that she required Dorothy to always call her Mrs. Witson, not by her first name with which she always called Dorothy. This Mrs. "W" is not to be confused with the Miss Walker (an only child and "old maid school teacher") who Dorothy also cleaned for. Just before she died, Miss Walker gave Dorothy a beautiful Christmas cactus which yearly blooms for Dorothy's November birthday, instead.

Of all the Cheyenne families Dorothy worked for, she only worked for two black families. First there was Judy, the beauty-operator. Second, there was Dr. Haynes. While Dorothy worked for his family, or even when he sees her now, Dr. Haynes continues to tease Dorothy about marrying him. He would say if both of them outlived their current spouses, that "she was so good at cleaning and frying foods that they would have marry, so she could clean and fry for him."

One of Dorothy's favorite working relationships and special family friends is the Murrays. She continues to work there now. During the past thirty-five years that Dorothy has worked for this family, the children all graduated from high school and completed some college, the father has died, and seven of the eight children have married. (In fact, Dorothy helped with the weddings of all but two of the seven married ones. One, she was too sick to attend but "saved the cake." The last, and favorite, child left and was married in Casper, instead of Cheyenne.) During those years, the Murrays have also gone from no married children to so many grandchildren that Dorothy has lost track of most of them. She does know that the first grandson is now grown himself and is an attorney in California.

Through all these years that Dorothy has labored at the Peppermint (her name for the Murray's red and white painted) Ranch, she lunched with Barbara, the matriarch, each time she came. While eating, Dorothy shared stories of her life in the South, of being Black, and it was of these stories that gave birth to this book. Of these "many good days at the Ranch," Dorothy remembers many especially of Frontier Days, particularly of meeting the fancy dressed

Saloon girls of the Melodrama and the meticulous Thunderbird fliers. At home, she even now displays a signed Thunderbirds picture hanging in her entryway. Of the Thunderbird fliers she shares some secrets. First, all Thunderbird fliers must weigh the same, even though they are different men each year. Also, their uniforms must be so impeccably manicured that the fliers' hats can spin on their heads and their Air Force uniforms ping. Finally, these fliers must be of near-genius intelligence which also radiates from their speech. Their manners too must match. Year after year, their extraordinary kindness was displayed by volunteer demonstrations to Dorothy. Yearly, one or more would come back to the kitchen offering to help cook or clean for her, so she could relax. She, of course, declined.

The Murrays, spiritual people and exceptional friends, promised Dorothy to be true to her even on the Other Side. However, Barbara Murray has often reminded

Dorothy that there is "No cleaning of the Pearly Gates, Dorothy." There "we will both have a rest and you will not have to toil, anymore." Many other religious Blacks have fantasized of the promised break Heaven offers. "Those rebby types, what do they think, anyway…When we get to the Spirit World, do they think colored people are going to be writing on their tables, pouring their tea…I think some of them are in for a big surprise. They're going to be pouring tea for me" (Delaney 16).

Dorothy is still currently employed by many other grateful families, many of whom she has also worked for a number of years. One of these families is the Dinneens of the Buick fame. Mr. Dinneen is gone but Dorothy still cleans for his wife, biweekly. Dorothy also still cleans for the Rowlands every other Tuesday. (On Monday and Wednesday evening, she cleans the Trophy Building with her sister, Leola.) Interestingly, we, the Dobsons, are the other Tuesday, opposite the Rowlands.

More about us, the Dobsons, there are six of us in all. However, when Dorothy first came to work for us, there were only four. Our twins were born and have grown up with Dorothy coming to see us every other Tuesday. Our oldest is now, as Dorothy describes "a mature, young lady," our boys, "gentlemen," and our other daughter, "precious." I am the Kris that "don't know how much good you do," and my husband "the good Mormon doc." It was because of "Doc Joe" that Dorothy came to work for us nearly ten years ago. As already mentioned, Daughter-in-law Senovia, was at the time working with my husband, and we needed help keeping up with all our little ones. Through all the years, the greatest compliment Dorothy ever gave our family was recently when she and I were talking about this book and racism. Without solicitation, Dorothy replied by saying, "No, your children are not racist. They were not taught to be. At your home is one of the few places, outside of my home, where I am truly free."

We like to tease that it helps Dorothy's friendship with our family because we love her Sweet Potato Pies, made especially for us on occasions such as Thanksgiving and Christmas, so much. I am equally impressed that she loves my "authentic Macaroni and Cheese" and lets me make it for her because I am the only "little white girl she knows who can cook soul food."

"Get Da Steppin!"

Speaking of authentic Southern cooking, Dorothy, herself, tells of baking possum with sweet potatoes, making sweet water from sugar water and corn bread, and cooking collard greens and chitlins: fried pig intestines. Being from the plantation, Dorothy claims to never have learned to cook much meat, per se. "James Sr. was the one any good at cooking meat." She added, "Meat, what's meat? I'm from a plantation, remember?" However, recently, when she went to visit her sister, still living in the South, they did eat "regular meat." In fact for breakfast, she had two meats, bacon and sausage, along with two starches, rice and grits. In contrast to these Southern entrees, she said, "Tianna, in Wyoming, I must teach potatoes." Dorothy's kitchen, itself, what's more speaks of cooking with its wall hangings and sense of humor. One, "this kitchen closed due to illness... I'm sick of cooking." Second, "I'm not a fast cook... I'm not a slow cook... I'm a half-fast cook."

When asked, many of Dorothy's loved ones, (all of which have undoubtedly spent numerous hours in Dorothy's kitchen), spoke of food or their favorite meals. First, Keith told that his favorite Sunday dinner was lasagna (maybe not so Southern) and sweet potatoes. Also, Pernisha told of learning to make "wonderful boxed cakes" and added the following: "As a teenager, my grandpa would pick me up from school, or I'd ride the bus. Whenever I got home, my grandma would have something cooked or baked to eat. The house was always filled with aromas of something, whether it was food or cleaning supplies. I always came home to a smell. My grandpa made sure there was food in the house, and my grandma made sure to cook it. My grandma was always the type to have a snack or a small meal prepared when her kids or grandkids came home from school. I assume she was taught that as a child. Even, today, it is still done."

Additionally, granddaughter, Ashley, said, "You'll find that Dossy spends a good portion of time in the kitchen. Aunt Leola, her sister, and a few others of my grandma's visitors sit at the table. Sipping their drinks, they smart off the latest news about the block. On the back porch the children, or 'chillins,' as Grandma calls them run and play. Laughter of little voices soars through the air, circling from the front to the back of the house. Fridays and Sundays are when the swarm of people come all wanting to get a little of Grandma's Southern cooking. We've all heard the term 'soul food,' quite frankly that is what makes Dossy's food so good: the soul. Boy, can she cook: homemade macaroni, greens, ribs, and catfish. Breakfast includes ham, grits, eggs, and then a choice of cereal. Grandma gets up at five o'clock in the morning to prepare breakfast. I remember waking to tantalizing smells filling my nostrils. All can hear her, rustling around in the kitchen, along with crackling of eggs. Ham slices sizzle on the stove, as the clatter of a wooden spoon hits plastic to stir up orange juice. Once you enter the kitchen from your sleep, the smells hit like a tidal wave. Just what more can an empty tummy ask for? Supper calls for even more preparation time. Grandma calls all the females into the bright, yellow kitchen to help. 'Get da stepping, Ashley start snapping dem beans for grandma,' she squawks in her Southern drawl. At meal time, we gather on the back porch and feast in our soulful gifts. Afterwards, the girls once again help out Grandma. When we enter the kitchen for clean up, the smell of barbeque sauce is still lingering in the air. Then, Dossy makes sure her kitchen is spotless before bedtime, and she also makes sure she doesn't get it that way by herself."

"It's a Blessing to Help"

Because of her cooking, willingness to share anything, and her openness to house and hearth, it is no wonder that Dorothy always says, "It's a blessing to help, got a long way to go, though." Because of the number of people, from all races, creeds, and nationalities, which Dorothy has touched over the years, it is impossible to mention them all. However, here are a few of the written comments given to me in response to my inquiry about her friendships and acquaintances: Mary Peterson called Dorothy "My friend, whom I hold dear in my heart." Kathy Kooce said, "Sister Dorothy has always encouraged me to hold on to Jesus. I have to. For Jesus is my only strength. My love for Him will not ever fade away." Frances Presbury from three blocks away wrote the following:

Letter to Dorothy:
August 6, 2008

Mrs. Hayes
I met Mrs. Hayes (Dorothy) in 1966. (Interestingly, the year the author was born.)
Dorothy is the same now as she was then. She always is a person who listens when you speak, and she is a very hard working lady.
My family and I truly love her. She will do whatever she can for you. Dorothy has been a blessing to my family and me. She has a saying I quote, "If I can't help you, I sure am not going to harm you."
Dorothy is truly a child of God. She is a hard worker in the church and out. She loves the Lord.
Sister Hayes, you keep on keeping on.
We love you.
Sister Frances Presbury

(P.S. We are all so proud of Mother Hayes and support her book and legacy.
—Grandson, Frances Presbury)

"Never Had it to Miss"

Having so many kind friends, generous employers, and thrifty ways, Dorothy, without shame, claims to not buy herself new, or rarely even, her own, clothes. If Dorothy does buy clothes, she purchases them from garage sales and "Goodwill." Without reservation, she also reiterated that she truly was not upset by not wearing new clothes because she "never had it to miss." She had grown up "being Black in the South," wearing hand-me-downs from the older children (as a middle one of eight), the entire family receiving most of their clothing first "from the White folks back on the Plantation." In reality, Dorothy's first new coat was at fifteen years of age. To this day, Dorothy continues to mostly wear hand-me-downs. However, she now gets them from whom she works for, other friends, and church associates. She has even been called "take whatever you get Mother" by her children and grandchildren. While researching this book, it was an employer who gave Dorothy the tape recorder to record the notes with. During the same time period, she also got a "new" knitted winter hat from her daughter's employer and a brown jumper from a church friend.

    Not all Black women are as accepting as Dorothy of hand-me-downs and the like. In fact, a church acquaintance of Dorothy's criticized her for wearing other people's (especially White people's) clothes. This woman claimed to be "too good for hand-me-downs, even if they are leather or brand new." Instead of being offended, Dorothy just concurred with the statement, "You shouldn't be running all around bad-mouthing your own kin" (Delaney 292). It did make her frustrated, though, that another "Black sister would work against, instead of, for her own." Maybe Dorothy's accepting and positive attitude is because, like her mother and grandmother before, she has always come to believe and recognize "What will be, will be."

When accused of being old-fashioned about many things, including having hand-me-downs, Dorothy just shrugged and said, "That's okay with me." In fact, she still believes, and has often proven that the "old ways" are at least as good, if not better than the "new ways." Dorothy, truthfully, is proud of many of these "old ways" and how they still seem to work better. Her daughter Kathy even teases that Dorothy could probably be a millionaire, today, if she had patented some of the "tricks of her generation." Particularly, when Crest and Colgate came up with the "white up strips" idea, everyone that knew Dorothy well enough, especially her children, knew those companies had just recreated one of Dorothy's (their mother's) old solutions. Kathy tells of while growing up when "a quick teeth clean" was required, Mom just told them to "take a clean cloth, wet it a little, rub it on our teeth, and then they would be instantly whitened. Then, we would be presentable for any who would now see our whiter grin. Sound vaguely familiar?"

On the other hand, Dorothy has "never lost out by taking hand-me-downs" from her employers, for she has always been so respected and loved by them. Her children and grandchildren agree by saying, "She's blessed and honored: always gets the most Christmas presents…Every

Christmas even until this day has more presents than anybody else in the family. This must also prove her reputation!" Pernisha even added, "My grandma and I would always receive the most presents. The front porch and a corner in the living room would be packed with presents. You would think it was only us in the family. My grandma would receive presents from everyone! All the people she worked for gave her BIG presents. Presents like coats, clothes, bread makers, bed comforters, new sets of dishes and cookware, stereos. That's just off the top of my head and not including before I was born. She is also said to be everyone's favorite aunt, so even her nieces and nephews give her presents. She never got anything cheap either. Guess she is loved by all!"

"Blood is thicker than Mud"

Speaking of Pernisha, the sickly preschooler, is now twenty-six and a mother, herself. Growing up in her grandparent's home, Pernisha obviously had a special relationship with Dorothy and James Sr. She particularly acknowledged her "Papi" (Grandpa) for being the only father "she really had" and promised him when he was near death that "finally, with God and you, I can succeed and won't let this family 'run into the ground.'" She even added the following, almost in his honor, after James Sr. passed on July 2, 2000: "We'd have these fishing and camping weekends often in the summertime until my grandfather was too sick to make frequent trips as such. Don't get it confused, we still did those sorts of things. To keep the tradition alive, we still go. It's just not the same without grandpa. I will never forget those trips because they were so often memorable. Every trip was never the same. We always had great times especially when we went fishing."

It was not only Pernisha who admired her grandfather. Similar recognition was shown to James Sr. as he lay in the hospital dying. The nurse that was assigned to him knew him well from the community and honored him by saying: "Jim Hayes was, and is, a good man to everyone." Dorothy could say little more than the best about her husband of more than fifty years, although she had to admit that James Sr. did have a drinking problem and some control issues because of it. However, she emphasized that drink never stopped her husband from "taking care of business." No matter what, even if he was drunk, he was always to work by seven a.m. and that is "how she survived."

In truth, James raised high above many of his ancestors in dealing with family addictions, including their drinking problems. Specifically, James Sr. may have looked like his dad physically, but in actions, he lived much superior to him in many ways. Particularly, and even though "blood may be thicker than mud," James outlived his father in more than just years. Because of the wandering eyes and spirit, James' father met an untimely death. Because James' father was having an affair with one of the twins that worked at his father's (James' grandfather's) Ten Cent Café, James's father was killed by a brick layer who was also interested in the same woman. James was later picked up, by the cop "walking the beat," to help identify his father who was left lying on sidewalk with a broken neck. James had to be dragged out of work midday, where he "cooked meat" at his Uncle's Quick Nickel Restaurant, unaware of what was even happening. Because of this situation, Dorothy concurs with her mama which said, "The first way around is the best way home…take the straight and narrow." Ironically, in spite of this entire situation, James Sr.'s mother (the murdered man's wife) continued to be, and "was always a saint to all," continuing on alone that "long, difficult life, as a widow." Additionally, proving as Dorothy's mother also said that "all people, innocent or not, are better off, if all people do it good, no half steps."

"Flying like an Eagle"

Dorothy, like James, had to, as told of before, overcome life-altering childhood experiences brought on by others' indiscretions. She even admitted that it took her into her now-advanced age to come to grips with many of them. Finally, Dorothy is able to "fly like an eagle." Hopefully, these positive changes came to pass partly because society moved from a less optimal past to a better future. Thus, as Brice F. Taylor said in 1960, "yesteryear many decisions were made which seemed undesirable and spineless. As we have grown older… we can see why these things were done and at what a high cost the individuals who were noble and strong enough to make them."

An impossibility, as much as Dorothy or James getting over their past, seems to many the unlikelihood of having a Black president. (Ironically, this also occurred concurrently with the writing of this book). The Black Delany sisters in their book Having Our Say, written in the

1990s, had conjectured: "I guess it will be a thousand years—probably never—before a colored person is elected president of the United States. Sadie disagrees with me. She says, 'There will be a Negro president someday.'...That reminds me of a song that White minstrels in blackface would sing to make fun of Negroes, back in the 1890s:

Oh my, what fun...In Washington
I bettya every coon...From coontown will be there
On my, what fun...In Washington
When the coon sits in that presidential chair...

See, I think White people would rather die than vote for a Negro president. I predict there will be a White woman president before there is a Negro president. If a Negro is elected president, that person will be a Negro woman."

Obviously, Dorothy and her family were very much involved in campaigning for the Barak Obama election. In actuality, Dorothy may have not met Barak Obama personally, but she had his and many other Democratic signs, particularly for Black candidates, in her yard over the years. With this, and her participation in yearly Martin Luther King Jr. celebrations, it becomes quite clear that Dorothy is not only accepting, but proud, of her Black heritage. She may not have heard any of Martin Luther King Jr.'s speeches personally, but she did meet Martin Luther King the third. Additionally, the rest of her family met all Martin Luther King Jr.'s children and his wife Coretta Scott King at a Democratic Party rally years ago in Denver. Furthermore, every Christmas, Dorothy's niece (Carey's daughter, who keeps in contact even though her father died in a Union Pacific Railroad injury in years past) buys Dorothy a stylized "Black Character" figurine from the South. Dorothy also has a neighbor who makes and displays Civil War characters every February for Black History Month. With this aging friend, Dorothy is only sad that her neighbor is showing her age enough to not be able celebrate this year's Black successes like she is.

Truthfully, Dorothy thinks "life's a blessing. Still got a long way to go…"

In fact, on June 12, 2009, Dorothy officially became a great-grandma when Pernisha gave birth to her son. Labor started that morning with pains and uncomfortable calls for "grandma." Grandma got to help Pernisha endure through the entire day until around 9:30 p.m. when the tiny (little over five pounds) Solomon (another boy "Bible-named" grandson) came. Uncle James and his disappearing act during the delivery quickly reminded Dorothy of her own husband James and his similar disappearance when Pernisha herself was delivered. At least, Solomon was not born at 1:00 in the morning. All are so glad for Solomon's safe arrival. Some even attribute his safe arrival (his mother was the sickly child, Pernisha) to the good family he is born into. After all, the saying goes that "when you're good, things work out good."

"I'm not a senior citizen…I'm a recycled teenager."

As is demonstrated by one of Dorothy's T-shirts, she does not feel, or act, as "old as she is." She could feel "maybe older and bolder than before," but not just old. Describing herself last year, she said she was "eighty-three years young." Many people believe this to be true because of how many tasks Dorothy still does. They say, including my children, that she does not look, or act, like someone in her eighties. Dorothy insists her physical well-being is just a "blessing from God for staying on the straight and narrow path and having a job to do."

Presently, Dorothy is also employed working with other "senior citizens." She sits Sunday evenings with an older shut-in. However, because this woman's mind is so alert, even though she is blind, Dorothy would have no complaints to be like her at her age (in her nineties). For everyone's information, Dorothy wants to work at the

"Home of the Elders" when she is too feeble to clean anymore. Who knows when that will be, though.

One of the strangest things for Dorothy at her age is comparing herself to others her own age. Just like the Delany Sisters she has often thought: "You know what I've been thinking lately? All those people who were mean to me in my life—all those rebby boys—they have turned to dust…We've outlived those old rebby boys! That's one way to beat them! That's justice! They're turning in their graves while …we are getting the last word…And honey, I surely do love getting the last word. I'm having my say, giving my opinion. Lord, ain't it good to be an American. Truth is, I never thought I'd see the day when people would be interested in hearing what old Negro women have to say. Life still surprises me. So maybe the last laugh's on me" (298 and 299).

Dorothy just seems to be "almost runnin' still." The almost being caused by a previously-broken foot, (had to learn to walk the stairs with the crutches before she went home), weakened eye sight for which she had surgery this year, and other minor health concerns. Pernisha stated the following about her grandmother's age: "Grandma hasn't changed with time. She's wiser if anything. Since her knee surgery, she just slowed down about five mph, but she still has more energy than anyone else in the family! Besides that, she has been the same all my twenty-seven years on earth."

However, it truly seems that the only changes to Dorothy's health over the years have been not much more than slight inconveniences to her and her doctor visits just chances to meet more people. Her list of doctors may be long but most seem to be her confidants, and food recipients, as much as they are her guides and health care providers. It was even the people at Physical Therapy, from this aforementioned broken foot, that suggested she "write a book." Dorothy does, however, miss the "privilege of giving blood" due to her weakened health conditions. She loved to give blood but "just can't now" because of the medication she is on. Truthfully, she admits giving blood was not probably as nice as the excuse to have thirty minutes to relax, have a cookie and juice, in addition to helping someone else. Paradoxically, one time after giving blood, Dorothy did fall asleep on the job. Fortunately, no one was home, so she could lay down for a little over an hour, wake up, finish her work, and no one would be the wiser that this day's work took a little longer than usual.

"Epilogue"

The year is now 2009. Dorothy James Hayes is no longer a naive Black adolescent so desperate to leave Mississippi. She is not even the fifteen-year-old that, because her mother was so strict, was terrified just watching her first movie afraid that "those men were going to get her" (meaning Joe Lewis and the men in top hats).

Nor is she the new bride in her twenties now, on the other side of her country, in Los Angeles, California: "Away from home for the first time, married, living with in-laws, and working in a totally different environment, one moving so fast and offering her lessons she would not have even thought of in Mississippi." Finally, she is no longer even the train contractor's wife just visiting Wyoming for employment. She became a pillar citizen in the city of Cheyenne and a vibrant part of the living fiber of that Wyoming community. Dorothy may still believe that Mississippi and Wyoming are as different as day and night in "everything from the people to the food, from politics to the ethics, and also from family discipline to up-bringing." However, through her years in both, she succeeded in making the mix of the two into a perfect blend.

As this book closes, we all start to feel like granddaughter, Ashley: "When it's time to leave Grandma's and head back to Washington, it becomes a sad event. Tears stroll down our faces as we try to squeeze the life out of each other. We pull out of the driveway and past the Frontier Days Fairground, again, heading for the highway. Gosh, will I miss that food and family. As we drive on, I am thinking about all the wonderful memories I can add of Grandma's house." However, we must realize that Dorothy does not want us to be sad as we close this book about her.

Instead, as on February 27, 1994, Dorothy's Denver nieces and nephew (Bertha's daughters and son) celebrated "Dorothy James-Hayes Day," so should we. May her life continue to celebrated by all who share her philosophies on life—moral integrity, family loyalty, and above all, racial love and equality. In her own words, Dorothy's only true desire was to be not "just a number, but someone that moved the world on." As the song says of this life, and even the next:

"The Train is Moving On"
The train is moving on, on, and on...The train is moving on, on, and on...And you got to reach your destination...The train is moving on, on, and on (repeat once)
 I looked down the road, I saw the train coming...I step on board and the train kept running...But you got to reach your destination
The train is moving on, on, and on...The train is moving on, on, and on...And you got to reach your destination...The train is moving on, on, and on
 You can talk about me as much as you please, the more you talk the more I'm gonna stay on my knees cause I got to reach my destination the train's moving on, on, and on.
If you get to heaven before I do , tell all my friends that I'm coming too cause I got to reach my destination...The train is moving on, on, and on.

Therefore, Dorothy would have us all (herself included) simply, "keep movin' on."

The End

Sources:

Carruth, Gorton with Raymond V. Hand, Jr. What Happened When: A Chronology of Life and Events in America. New York: HarperPerennial, 1989, 321-393.

Delany, Sarah L. and A. Elizabeth Delany with Amy Hill Hearth. Having Our Say: The Delany Sisters' First 100 Years. New York: Dell Publishing, 1994.

Fairclough, Adam. A Class of Their Own: Black Teachers in the Segregated South. Massachusetts: Belknap Press, 2007.

Frances Presbury. Letter to the biographed. 6 August 2008.

Forest Robin. "The Train is Moving On." Acoustically Speaking, 2008.

"Good-bye Mr. Fish." The Cosby Show: Season One. NBC. WNBC: New York: 27 September 1984.

Halvorson, Barry. "Crown, Portraits of Black Women in Church Hats." Black History. 17 March 2009 <www.journal-spectator.com/news/2008/0216/news/013>.

Hayes, James Granger Jr. Personal Interview. January 2009.

Hayes, Keith. Personal Interview. December 2008.

Hayes, Pernisha. Personal Interview. January 2009.

Hayes, Tianna. Personal Interview. January 2009.

Heaven's Grocery Store. Reading. Perf. Dorothy Hayes. October 2005.

Holy Bible, King James Version. USA: Intellectual Reserve, Inc, 1979.

Ibach, Kim and William Howard Moore. The Emerging Civil Rights movement: The 1957 Wyoming Public Accommodations Statue as a Case Study. 9 November 2008 <http://uwacadweb.uwyo.edu/Robertshistory/civil_rights_movement.htm>.

Judge, Sandra. "The Cleaning Lady from the Five Important Life Lessons." Email to the author. 8 January 2009.

Lee, Harper. To Kill a Mockingbird. New York: Grand Central Publishing. 1960.

Mitchell, Margaret. Gone with the Wind. New York: Macmillan, 1936, 578-579.

Quester, Brandon. "Church Honors its Genesis." Wyoming Tribune Eagle 19 October 2008: B1.

Rambo, Ashley Hayes. "Get Da Steppin!" English Essay. 16 October 2002.

Rambo, Kathy Hayes. Personal Interview. February 2009.

The Color Purple. Motion Picture. Dir. Steven Spielberg. Perf. Danny Glover, Oprah Winfrey and Whoopie Goldberg. Warner Brothers, 1985.

The Williams Brothers. Lyrics. "I'm Just a Nobody Trying to help Somebody." <u>Greatest Hits: Volume II</u>. 5 November 2008.
<http://www.allgosepllyrics.com/pritnwin.pp?id=666>.

About the Author:

Kirstin Dobson is a woman on a quest, fulfilling a lifelong dream; one who is lucky enough to tell of another woman who changed the world for herself, many others, and even me. Kirstin is also an English instructor in Cheyenne, Wyoming and a mother of four: Kristina, Joseph, Kathryn, and Jakob. She is also a long time employer and friend of the Hayes family, especially Dorothy. I (Kirstin) would like to thank all of you, particularly the Hayes family and especially, Dorothy, for allowing me the privilege to know you, and also to share these many experiences with you.

Made in the USA
Las Vegas, NV
27 February 2022